Cooking With Gas

Cooking With Gas
The Official Guide For Restaurant Startup and Operation

Luke V. Saucier, III

ISBN : 1-4196-3189-6

To order additional copies, please contact us.
BookSurge, LLC
www.booksurge.com
1-866-308-6235
orders@booksurge.com

Cooking With Gas

Table of Contents

The Holy Trinity in the restaurant business.

Let's get this party started.

My name is Delila. Tomorrow I will finally open the doors to my new restaurant *Delila's con Carne*. I am a sole proprietor. We experienced some delays during start up, but at least we will open during the Christmas holiday, which should be good for business. I am so excited.

I have never hired people before, but I think I've done okay. Actually I think I've done great! One of the star football players from nearby Central High School just happened to apply; he said that football season had just ended and he was looking for something to do, and I just couldn't help myself; the guy was so cute, I gave him the job right away! Later he brought a few of his teammates and friends along, and I gave them jobs too. They are all so cute. Also, there is a halfway house nearby with people who are in desperate need. They are kind of yucky, but I want to do what I can to help, so I employed a few of them as well. I haven't started training my staff yet because, to be honest, I think training is over-rated. And all that talk of "teams" and "teamwork?" Again, over-rated. That's just macho-man talk. Just give people a chance, and they will appreciate you and work hard for you. I don't have a manager to help run the operations for me, but I don't really see the need. I can handle everything myself. My refrigerator and freezer are stocked to the limit. I wasn't sure how much to order, so I ordered plenty of everything. That pesky insurance guy has been by a couple of times, but his prices for worker's compensation, general liability and so forth are just too high. I think I can wing it the first few months without insurance. If I'm careful, nothing will happen. I'm ready to open, actually over ready. I felt that I was ready some time ago, but I never knew I had to collect sales taxes for the county and city. I didn't know that to register with those taxing authorities I had to have an EIN, an Employer Identification Number. In fact I didn't even know what an EIN was. That caused me to backtrack and do a lot more legwork right when I thought we would open. Also, I never knew that I would have to have my plumbing and electrical systems inspected, so that took more time. Next, I had to be inspected by the health department prior to opening, and then, just when we again thought we were ready, a sign-off by the fire marshal was required. Guess who was on vacation? Finally we needed a certificate of occupancy. Nobody ever told me any of this was required. Also construction took much longer than expected, not to mention the fact that the cost of the job ran 50% above initial estimates. All of these things created further delays, and as a result I did lose a few of the people I hired, actually about half, but I think I'll be all right because I hired more than enough to start with.

I know I'm going to do well because of my location. I have always heard that if you locate near McDonald's, you will do well because they have already done all the feasibility studies for their sites and choose locations carefully, and here I am just across the street. Also I have been running a TV commercial for my grand opening for weeks now.

As my name suggests, my concept centers around beef. I'm going to sell burgers, steaks, and some Mexican dishes and a few BBQ beef dishes. My family and friends say I'm an excellent cook and I have some very good recipes. It's an easy homerun, I can't lose.

Good luck Delila.

Sometimes we don't know everything we need to know, and *we don't know that we don't know*. We think we know, but we don't. We don't know which questions to ask; we don't even know that there are questions we should ask.

When that is the case, you are the single greatest detriment to your own success. When we are young, and/or inexperienced, we don't hear words of sage advice; they roll off us like water off a duck's back. Then along comes life. Life doesn't care that you don't know. Like a deer in the headlights you are run down by the school bus of hard knocks. Often you begin to realize that there were questions you should have asked, but by then it's too late. You knew those two bright lights coming at you and the strange noise growing louder and louder weren't right, but you didn't get out of the way. You'll know next time — if there is a next time. This, my friend, is called experience. Experience teaches you that you don't know everything.

Delila never knew. She had a good recipe or two and thought all she had to do was hang out a shingle, open the doors and start cooking. But wait, it ain't that easy. There is so much more that goes into operating a successful restaurant and that's why I wrote this book.

Delila finally opened her restaurant. As expected, they were packed on that first day. But because there had been no real training, there was no coordination at all among her service staff, or between her service staff and the kitchen. Her employees did not seem to pull together as a team, and more than a few customers were unhappy. One or two were heard to say, as they were walking out, that they would never return.

As unbelievable as it may sound, on the first day a customer slipped and fell on a spilled drink in the entrance foyer and an employee, Amanda, fell in the kitchen too. Amanda said she was absolutely fine, though, and returned to work. Delila had meant to look after the customer who fell, but was distracted by other things. The customer left. When the dust finally settled on that first day, Delila was able to sit in her office and recollect. Sales were really good. She had run out of a few key items, but, oh well, another delivery was coming in two days. One thing was certain: she had plenty of hamburger meat. Strangely, she had not sold many burgers at all that day. She wasn't sure, but it was possible that maybe not even one burger had been sold all day. Maybe later she could dig through the tickets — if she could find them. They had taken orders by hand and used an old refurbished cash register like the ones Delila remembered fondly from her childhood. Come to think of it, a big stack of tickets had gone out with the trash, so she wouldn't be able to research whether or not any hamburgers had been sold. She could not believe how tired she was and this was just the first day. It had been tough, because she was actually much shorter on staff than she had anticipated, and it seemed that her high school boys had picked on the halfway house people a little, but maybe she was mistaken. Also, the halfway house employees, who frankly she did not much care for, were too slow, and her customers did not appreciate their hygiene. Josh, the high school football star, had been her saving grace all day. It seemed he was just where she needed him at all times; he was reliable and so cute too. Thank God. It occurred to her that she might have waited until a little closer to actual opening to do her hiring, but oh, she was so tired.

Well, things didn't improve the rest of the week. The business still came in droves, far more than she was prepared to handle. The coordination—no, you couldn't call it that—the lack of coordination among the staff was appalling, and oh yeah, her initial hunch had been correct: there was definitely friction between those nasty halfway homeless people and the high school students. In one short week it had grown into an all out war and the sad thing was it had caused the loss of two of her better employees. She tried to placate, to mediate, but all to no avail; the harder she tried the worse the morale. She noticed she had to fight her own distaste for the halfway house people. What made matters really worse was that she had actually heard, with her own ears, grumblings from these people. THEY seemed unappreciative of her efforts to help them and made snide comments about helping her to get rich and the paltry amounts they were paid. They seemed to work even slower, if that was possible. This really hurt Delila's feelings and made her mad. As if that wasn't enough, now Amanda was complaining that her back was bothering her from the fall in the kitchen and that she was going to the hospital to get it checked out.

Meanwhile, business was good, but Delila was truly exhausted and was remotely aware that this factor might be affecting her decision-making abilities. Being out of those key items had seemed to compound her problems. Delila could not seem to get a handle on what items to order, or in what quantity. It seemed everyone wanted only the things she was out of. Hamburger meat was absolutely not moving. No burger sales, no Mexican food sales. She had made little progress on saving order tickets. Everything was moving so fast and she was having trouble containing it all. Staffing issues were becoming very troublesome with three employees out and no time to hire new ones. Actually, staffing was really critical, but again Josh had been her savior all week. She had good feelings about him and he was so handsome and big and strong, which had been very useful for the work that needed to be done.

By the end of her first month Delila was wondering what had ever made her want to be in the restaurant business. Nothing was going well. She was perpetually out of items she needed, but had had to throw away a large quantity of hamburger meat that had gone bad. She had finally figured out what was wrong there; in anticipation of her opening, the McDonald's across the street had lowered the price on the Quarter Pounder to 79 cents. Also Burrito Mundo, the Mexican buffet two doors down, had lowered all of their prices as a holiday special and that was generating a lot of buzz throughout town. The result: no burger sales and no Mexican food sales. Delila felt really stupid that she hadn't caught on to these things earlier; there may have been some way she could have responded. Her employee situation, well, she couldn't even stand to think about it. All she had wanted to do was help, and those damned, smelly, inept, halfway people had really pushed her over the edge. They really seemed to resent both her and the high school kids. Their grumblings had gotten louder about all the money SHE was making and now she was even hearing that from her high school kids.

Funniest of all, though, was the fact that she had thought that she was making a whole bunch of money. Delila labored under some false assumptions about profit. With all the business she had, she could not figure out where her money was going, but it was definitely going. For example, she noticed that she was paying an awfully large percentage of her revenues to her employees and that there were payroll taxes on top of that, something she had not even known about, and the aggravating forms she now had to fill out to make her payroll tax deposits; no one had ever told her about that either, but, come to think of it, she had never asked. And where was she supposed to find the time to do this? And sales taxes! She didn't even have the money at the moment to pay them. Also, food was costing an enormous amount and yet she was continually out of certain items and had too many of others. Amanda had become a big problem; her hospital bills were coming in and Delila had no idea how she was going to pay them or even if she had to. And now, a letter has arrived from an attorney representing the lady who had fallen in her foyer—she was being sued. She had completely forgotten that incident. Oh my God, when is it gonna end, she thought to herself.

A couple other things weighed on Delila's mind as she sat in her chair recalling her first month. In her mad dash from one thing to the next throughout those busy days, she had forgotten one very important group of people: her customers. They came, so she just did whatever needed to be done, but now as she thought about it, she realized that the service her customers received was horrible. There was no set way to approach a table and she had not really formulated any strategy for handling complaints; it seemed—no, her employees were definitely doing a poor job of it. She realized that people were not returning for subsequent visits to her restaurant. She resolved to think on this some more and do something about it real soon.

The other thing on her mind was that night last week. It had involved Josh, who had continued to be her saving grace. One night, late, after a long day, she and Josh were the only ones left in the restaurant and they were standing in the office talking. She wasn't sure exactly what it was she had intended, but she knew she wanted to say something about just how much she appreciated Josh's help. She had laid her hand ever so delicately upon his bicep.

It was over in a flash. She wasn't even sure how it happened and she had not meant for it to happen, but one thing was for sure, she had done nothing to stop it. They had sex in her office.

Now the holiday season was ended and Josh had gone back to school just when she needed him the most. That meant he couldn't or wouldn't work when she wanted him to and this was causing big friction between them. She was angry all the time and he seemed surly and non-communicative. She counseled him often when they were alone in her office and she really had to work at not yelling at him. Worst of all Josh had said that he felt he was being harassed and had even threatened to hire a lawyer. HE WAS BEING HARRASSED AND IT WAS HER THAT WAS BEING GOOD TO HIM was all Delila could think. And, lord, she was tired.

Okay, Okay, enough already. I know that you, gentle reader, can't take anymore of this nightmare. Thankfully this is a cautionary tale filled with just *some* of the things that can go wrong in this business when you lack experience. Give it six more months and Delila will be out of business. By that time she will do anything to be released from the hell she has found herself in: file for bankruptcy or beg to go to debtor's prison and work on the chain gang breaking rocks all day. If you think this business is easy, think again. And if this scenario scares the hell out of you, then good, for it should.

Delila's failure was Ignorance and its twin Hubris. She had failings at every level of management, and, at the end of just one month, was completely entangled in a web of her own making. All of this proceeded from the assumption that this undertaking would be a walk in the park; never dreaming that maybe there were questions she should ask. The restaurant business is far and away the most complex type of business to own and operate. Volumes could be filled on the details and complexities, the nuance and finesse, of this business. This little book is just an introduction.

As can be seen in this little vignette, too much business can be as destructive as too little; Delila was right about her location, and her advertising worked. In many ways she was a victim of her own success. Let's talk briefly here about Delila's major shortcomings; the following chapters will handle them in more depth.

- From the beginning Delila's assumptions about employees were incorrect. Her criterion for hiring was exactly wrong. She hired from feelings, on a whim, people she thought were cute or that she misguidedly wanted to "help." She hired people from backgrounds that were too divergent, and, as a result, had an all out war of conflicting interests, needs and personalities on her hands with her workplace as the battleground. One of her worst mistakes was hiring people who were desperately needy. (See chapter 7)
- Her distaste for her halfway house employees was always obvious to everyone but herself. Those employees felt shame and took it out on her customers through the snide remarks they made. This is known as passive aggressive behavior. (See chapter 7)
- Delila was never a leader, and you must be a leader in order to garner the respect of others. In turn you must respect your employees. Where mutual respect exists, morale will be high.   (See chapter 7)
- She hired prematurely and had not adequately researched what opening a restaurant entails; as a result she had delays, during which she lost valuable employees. (See chapters 7, 8, 9, 10)
- She never adequately anticipated competition. (See chapters 1, 2, 6)
- She did not see the need for professional management. (See chapter 10)
- She did not have systems in place for anything: training, ordering, tracking sales, financial statements, customer approach, recovery strategy for unhappy customers, preventing accidents both on the job and to her customers. (See chapters 5, 6, 8, 9, & 10)
- She was dismissive of training and teamwork. (See chapter 7)
- Delila failed to keep written reports and to document

the two slips and falls on her first day of business. (See chapters 10, 13)

- She failed to provide proper insurance coverage (See chapter 10):
  - Worker's comp.
  - General liability
  - Fire
  - Flood insurance
  - Business interruption
- Delila failed to have a unique or "core" product that would differentiate her from the crowd. (See chapter 1)
- She forgot her most important group of people: her customers. And even when she realized this, when she had this incredible epiphany, she resolved to think about it later. She procrastinated. (See chapter 8)
- She had no idea of the tremendous costs of unchecked labor or food. (See chapters 8, 9)
- Never did she research a Point of Sale (POS) system that might have helped her in many ways. (These machines have come a long way from the days of the old cash register.) (See chapters 9, 11)
- She is a sole proprietor, so now Amanda and the customer who fell in her foyer will come after her personal assets, including bank accounts, stocks, bonds, home, car—everything. Every asset Delila owns is now on the line. (See chapter 4)
- Delila was unreasonable about her prospects for success. There is never a guarantee of success even if you have great sales. Success is a function of operating correctly, building sales and controlling costs. (See chapters 2, 8, 9 & 10)•
- Not only did everyone else assume that every penny coming in was her profit, Delila thought so too. She knew she would have to pay rent and light bills and such, but then thought everything else was gravy. She

had never really given expenses any real thought. (See chapter 5)

- Delila counseled an employee of the opposite sex alone in her office while angry. She failed to have a witness. (See chapter 10)
- She made important business decisions while tired. (You don't make your best decisions when you are tired.)
- And finally, she did the unspeakable with Josh. It only happened once, but it will open a Pandora's Box of problems for her. (See chapters 7, 10)

This might seem like a nightmare that could never happen to you, but believe me, all of these things happen every day in business; there is plenty of Ignorance and Hubris to go around. Don't let this be you. Take my advice: Follow the words of this book and educate yourself further on the many facets of the restaurant business <u>before</u> you get started. Also, use www. cookingwithgas.net as a resource.

What Delila lacked was experience in management. Good management is all about planning and never happens by accident.

The rest of this book is dedicated to keep you from being Delila.

Introduction

*C*ooking With Gas: The Official Guide to Restaurant Start-ups and Operation"* is written for the entrepreneur who is thinking of opening his or her own restaurant. Whether you have been in the business for years or are contemplating becoming a first time restaurateur, there is something in this book for you. You need this book, and I think the prelude to this book showed you just some of the reasons why. Make *Cooking With Gas* your constant companion.

The expression *"Cooking With Gas"* suggests affirmative, positive momentum, and that is what I hope to impart to you. My years and experience in the restaurant business provide me with unique perspective that will benefit you in your operations; in over 30 years in this business, I have worked every possible position from dishwasher to owner; and I still do. Along the way, I picked up a B.S. in Accounting.

It is my mission to see you succeed. Indeed, I succeed when you succeed; to that end I will do all that I can to help you. I have been nurturing this book for many years and am glad to finally see it come to fruition. It is the product of a lifetime at the frontline; on that frontline I have had a lot of excitement and fun, but I have also had my share of jolts, and maybe I can spare you a few of the latter. Not found in this book is advice on which tables and chairs to buy or what air freshener scent you should use in your restroom; there are other books out there for that. This book is devoted to business set-up and the actual operations of your restaurant. What you will find in this book are subjects ranging from business organization to financial statements, functions of management to risk management. Our website www.cookingwithgas.net also includes tools to assist you in the start-up and day-to-day operation of your restaurant, from worksheets that will help you improve the skills set forth in this book, to important spreadsheets for tracking your daily sales, cumulative weekly sales and labor and food costs. These spreadsheets are not fancy, but sufficiently simple and straight forward to get the job done. You will also will find information on Corporation or LLC formation with links to every state's secretary of state. If small wares are what you're looking for we've got 'em, and be sure to check out the cool *Cooking With Gas* products. Check the Lagniappe section for our newsletter and quote of the day.

Let's take a look at the results of numerous studies conducted through the years on why businesses fail. Studies by organizations from Dunn & Bradstreet to The Small Business Association agree on the No. 1 reason for business failure. Can you guess what it is? Here's a hint: It's not lack of capital, that's the No. 2 reason why businesses fail. You guessed it. The No. 1 reason businesses fail is because of the lack of management knowledge and experience.

Do you possess the skills and experience in your field of endeavor; in this case the restaurant business? How about management experience: hiring, training, firing, record keeping, a familiarity with the federal and local laws governing the same? Do you have a working knowledge of financial management, accounting, financial statements and marketing plans? What are your ideas for cost controls? How about pricing? Got a handle on insurance and what types of coverage you might need? Do you know what records to keep, how to keep them and for how long? I know, I know it seems overwhelming, and yet, if you start your business without at least an introduction to these things, you will fail too. These are the reasons that 95% of all new business ventures fail. Sure, start-up capital is important, and, when things go bad, that's where everyone points the finger, but the real culprit in business failure is lack of knowledge and experience. The truth is perhaps just a little too personal and cuts to the quick, and I propose to share what I know from my years in this business and perhaps help you avoid that pain.

If you have an idea for a business that you are sure will work, America offers the entrepreneur more and greater opportunities than any other nation on earth. We are a nation of small business owners and our numbers are growing every day. Small business is by far the greatest employer in the United States and offers great financial rewards when run correctly. This book is a no-nonsense introduction to business formation and the protections offered by proper business organization. *Cooking with Gas* will guide you through the choice of business organization types, setting your mission statement, principles of management, the human resources function and necessary paperwork, and provide a brief introduction to financial statements. The goal of *Cooking with Gas* is to help you understand that starting your own restaurant is a challenging prospect offering brutal hours, low or no profit margins for the first year or two even when done right, but after you read this book, if you still think you want to open your own restaurant, then I want to help you do it right.

Throughout *Cooking with Gas* you will find information blocks called Quickfax. Quickfax will outline the main points in the briefest possible manner for easy digestion. This is the stuff you need to know and to put into practice where applicable.

Welcome and enjoy Cooking With Gas: The Official Guide to Restaurant Start-up and Management.

My First Thank You Is To My Wife, Kelley, For Her Resolute Support Of Me Through This Project, And For Making Our Life Together Wonderful. She Is The Editor Of My Manhood. A Special Thanks To My Editors-in-chief Bettie Marshall And Mark Judson For Their Indispensable Help. Thank You To My Brother Jason For His Enthusiasm And Support. Also, Thanks To Ed Moise, Jim Serra And Della Rose.

In Memory Of My Mother, Elizabeth Lee Saucier.

Chapter 1

To Franchise or Not

Are you going to operate a franchise or build a from-the-ground-up venture of your own? What's the difference? Many ask that question, and I will attempt to answer it here. Both have pros and cons, but in most cases the pros favor the franchise.

While visiting your uncle Fredtedjimmyjackjohn, he took you to Piggy's Smokehouse, his favorite little BBQ joint, with its incredible BBQ sauce unlike any you ever tasted; cool, rustic décor with exposed wooden beams; natural wood everywhere; trophy game heads on all the walls and the neat paper towel dispenser at the table that was "hands free." You were so smitten with the place that you immediately wanted to open one in your hometown. When you asked the waitress, you were informed in the affirmative, yes, they do franchise! Now what the hell does that mean? It means this: providing you can write the check up front for the franchise fee—an amount somewhere between $1,000 and $50,000 (probably closer to the latter)—and providing you meet their net worth and liquidity test (cash in bank) requirements, you can start looking for a location for your own Piggy's in your hometown. When you call Piggy's corporate office for further information, you are mailed the franchise circular; a tome thicker than the Bible, with everything you ever wanted to know about Piggy's. It takes an army of lawyers to figure this thing out, but basically it spells out the company history, past and present management, any judgments, litigations or bankruptcies, past or present. The circular details costs to you in the form of the up-front franchise fee and royalties from sales; it also details projected costs of building and equipment. Obligations on the part of the franchisee (you) to the franchisor (the Piggy's corporation) and vice versa are detailed. The circular might also detail the demographics required to support a Piggy's. For example, 75,000 people with an annual household income of $45,000 living in a three-mile radius may be required to support a Piggy's franchise. A great site for demographic information is the U.S. Census Bureau website at Factfinder.census.gov. Also, most public or university libraries should have demographic information.

If you decide to become a franchisee, you will have to conduct your business to the exact specifications of the company as laid out in its circular and operations manual. If you think you are going to do a Piggy's franchise but improve it, think again. Every aspect is laid out, and when you sign the franchise agreement, a contract between you and the franchisor, you agree to operate exactly as outlined. Any deviation may be considered a breach and put you in violation of your agreement. If you continue in violation, you will, among other things, lose the right to do business as Piggy's and you don't want that.

Here's the gist: the things you first liked about Piggy's—its delicious recipes and rustic décor—are the things they want to preserve and duplicate; they have already done the work and they cannot afford to have franchisees off changing any aspect of the business, not even the smallest detail. Piggy's Smokehouse has to be exactly the same in Bangor, Maine, as it is in San Antonio, Texas. If you think you can operate within those restrictions, you might make a good franchisee.

On the other hand, if you would chafe under the yoke of such oppressiveness, you might be more in the mold of a do-it-yourselfer. There's nothing wrong with that either; just come at it with your eyes wide open and be well aware of the dangers that face you. Don't let them cripple you; just be aware. See the comparisons of franchise versus do-it-yourself below.

Typically, with a franchise, you purchase the rights to a certain territory; for example: "The entire state of New Hampshire," or "the southwest corner of the state of Arkansas comprised of the counties of...." The reason this is important is that no other person can open a Piggy's in your territory. Each company is different, and you will want to have a very clear understanding of this fact going in because some franchises grant the same territory to more than one franchisee and may even open a corporate store within your territory. Imagine trying to compete with the resources of a corporation! I don't know why a company would do that because it seems at its core to be defeating the purpose, but regardless, these are things you need to know up front.

Let's take a look at advantages of franchise versus ground-up ventures.

Franchise:

Advantages

Name recognition. Successful recipes and décor. Support, training & training materials. Negotiated contracts for better pricing with vendors. Territory ownership. Help in choosing location. National marketing (with bigger franchises). Menus, signage, buildings (identity) are all created for you

Disadvantages

Royalties and advertising costs. Corporate insistence on operating by-the-book; (this is a matter of personal preference-some people don't like to be told what to do and how to do it all of the time.) There are some franchises that do not offer adequate services. It is up to you to do your research and ensure that you will receive adequate services for your investment.

Ground-up:

Advantages

Autonomy; doing "your own thing." No franchise fee. Small, "mom and pop" feel.

Disadvantages

Many of the kinks are not worked out. No name recognition. Unproven/untested recipes

Higher pricing for the same commodities as your franchise competitor. The challenge of creating your "brand" and creating graphics, menus, signs etc. Your choice of location could be disastrous

It is up to you to decide which business format appeals to you. New businesses start every day and many are successful, so it really comes down to what fits your personality.

Either way you go, you will work hard. You will face competition, and that is something you need to think long and hard about. Here's why: if you are entering a mature market with a product similar to that of your competitor's, let's say hamburgers for example, and you have worked so hard and risked it all on your venture, at this critical juncture, when you are most vulnerable, the hamburger dude across the street is going to start giving hamburgers away below cost and his cost is lower than yours because he's a franchise guy. He is well established and he can afford to do it; it's legal and that's business. It's a slug in the gut when your attention is elsewhere, but this punch will knock more than the wind out of you, because by the time you realize what has happened, it may already be too late. It will happen; I've been there, done that. You got this important point? *Now You Are Cooking With Gas!!! (NYCWG!)* Remember: Eyes Wide Open! This is stuff you need to know.

It is particularly important when you are a go-it-alone operation that you find a niche and some distance. Create an identity and try to have a unique core product and be faithful to that core product; after all, that is the way all those franchise organizations got started in the first place. After 30 years in this business, I truly admire those that have succeeded against the odds and it is my intent to help you succeed also!

In the end, though, I think you can see that the odds favor the franchise concept. Well, that's about it for this subject. Now that we've got that out of the way, it's time you started looking for a place to settle down.

Chapter 2

Location, Location, Location

There is a well-worn maxim in business that the three most important factors to a business's success are Location, Location and Location. You've heard it a million times, but now that you are considering your own business, it needs to take on a whole new meaning. First of all, if this book teaches you nothing else, I hope you learn that in the restaurant business, at least, there is a lot more that goes into making a business successful than just location. You may have the greatest location in the world, but if you are not executing in all areas, that won't matter. People won't come. Conversely, you can find great restaurants, as busy as all get-out, in horrible locations in every city across America.

But it is true that location is important, so let's get to it. Before you do anything, you will need information on which to base your decision making. The main question we need to answer is: what is the real cost of the location? To answer that, you need to answer the following questions:

- Does the location offer sufficient customer base?
- Does the demographic want what you're selling?
- Does the location offer sufficient employee base?
- Is there public transportation nearby?
- Does the location offer reasonable flow of traffic and ease of entry/exit of your site?
- Is any road work on the plans for the near future?
- What are the zoning regulations of your site? How about signage?

- Is your municipality business-friendly or will you be strangled with regulations and fees?
- What kinds of property taxes will you face?
- Is the area easily serviced by suppliers?
- What about politics? Is there some inducement today, such as an "Enterprise Zone" to get you in that building, which could evaporate tomorrow with a change in lawmakers? If so, how would that affect your bottom line?
- Will your location possibly face the exercise of "eminent domain" at some future date?
- Is the population of your city stagnant? Declining? Growing? If it is growing, what directions is it growing in, and are you going to be a part of that growth, or will your location be left to wither, slowly and painfully, on the vine?

So you have a great idea for a hip-hop coffeehouse called "Momma's Fashizzel — Coffee with Sizzle" featuring an edgy, jagged atmosphere with lots of maroons and browns and blacks, strobe lights, rap music and high voltage caffeinated drinks. It's a stimulant to all the senses, and you're gonna plunk it down right in the middle of a retirement community in Scottsdale, Arizona. You love your idea so much that you are going to try to make it work. The area has a suitable level of affluence, and you live nearby; you have found the perfect site for $4,400 per month with a $1,600 CAM (although you're not sure what that means); you just know it'll work. I've got a better idea: you mail me the $300,000 large, and go, right now, and check yourself into the nearest center for those who are chronically out of touch with reality and may have had just a little too much of that high octane coffee. You are a danger to yourself and your financial well-being if you don't deal in reality. What you are suffering from here is a case of the "new-car-smell-syndrome." Take a pill and sleep this one off and wake up tomorrow ready to do your homework.

You can't shove a square peg into a round hole. No matter how much your idea appeals to you, you don't count. It's what the customer wants. Get that through your head. You have to match the restaurant concept to the audience. Take that same concept and place it in a suburban strip center with lots of teenagers living nearby and you might have yourself a home run. What you need to have is congruence between customer and concept. Often, when we are infatuated with an idea, it is very hard to see its downsides.

Now that you have slept that off, you realize what a crazy idea it was. Not only would those who live nearby have disdain for your place, but no kids live nearby who could have staffed the place. Today, as you are driving by yesterday's dream site, you also notice that the median makes it impossible to make a left turn into the site, so that a large percentage of people traveling on that side of the road would drive on by; very few would make the u-turn to get back to your place. How could you have missed that!? you ask yourself. Not only that, but while filling up your tank across the street, the attendant tells you the city is getting ready do some work on the road. The project would take two years and involve tearing up and laying new road one section at a time. Silently, as the breeze blows in your hair, you thank God you didn't sign that lease. The important question here, now that you are a little more rational, is how you missed several important points that would have had a very negative impact on your business. Let me suggest that we are sometimes blinded by our visions; our eyes glaze over and our hopes and dreams put us in denial. When that big meanie called reality comes to call, we shove him away, sometimes forcefully, because it is so much nicer to live in that dream world. I don't want to beat a dead horse, but I hope I have made this point sufficiently clear. There are no guarantees that any site will be great, but you can know with a fairly high level of certainty when a site won't work. There are, however, many things you can do to maximize your chances.

Not a mile away, in the other direction, but equally close to your home, is just such a strip mall and it has a space that's perfect. There is a Starbuck's down the road and you can't believe how busy the place is when you go in there. The atmosphere is vanilla, the coffee is mediocre and the place has nothing on you; just wait till they get a load of Momma's Fashizzel; you are going to blow the roof off!

Now you are working with a realtor, and, by doing some homework, you have learned a lot more about real estate and have realized just how lucky you are that you didn't sign that lease: Your realtor pointed out that here the roads are new and wide and easily maneuverable for deliveries. You had already noted that there is no median, so left turns into this site are a breeze; the site you had been previously looking at was a planned community with narrow roads and limited ingress and egress. Also the realtor has taught you about signs. The previous location had heavy restrictions on signage, such as how tall your sign could be and what it could and could not look like. Also, you would have had to get approval for any paint colors on your building etc., etc. ad nauseam, and you never had any idea there were such restrictions; but that's okay, this community is much more business-friendly; there are still restrictions, but they aren't nearly as stringent. Your realtor has also shared with you the growth patterns of the area. Your previous location was actually moving slowly from stagnant to declining in population, whereas this community has seen steady growth of families with teenage kids, attracted by the two Blue Ribbon high schools in the area, and every indication is that the growth will continue for the foreseeable future. So you will have both an employee base and a customer base who will be very attracted to your concept. You are very pleased with rent, which is $2,500 with a $1,000 CAM. Previously you hadn't understood what CAM was, so you asked your realtor to explain it. She told you that it stands for Common Area Maintenance (CAM), a monthly fee that every tenant in the strip center pays as his shared portion of the maintenance expenses for the center, including insurance, taxes, trash removal, outdoor maintenance etc., and that it is pro-rated according to each site's percentage of the whole complex. That makes perfect sense and finally that mystery is solved.

As you look up and down the road from your new site you see

that all of the big name fast food outlets are there. Your realtor explains this as a phenomenon called "clustering effect." A big name such as McDonald's researches the area to determine if there are favorable factors such as a stable, abundant customer base with sufficient incomes, stable employee base, and reasonable wages in the area. If these factors are satisfactory, they then set up shop in the neighborhood; soon many big and not so big names follow. She further explains that there are benefits and drawbacks to this arrangement. Some of the benefits are the fact that more sites drive more traffic, which begets more business which further drives traffic; when one restaurant is packed, patrons may not want to wait, so they go to the restaurant next door or across the street. This is called "spillover." It is also easier for vendors to service you here. Some of the drawbacks are that when an area over-develops, that same traffic that was good before can become a nuisance; people can't get in, or, more importantly, can't get out, of a certain parking lot as easily as they once could, and as a result they don't pull in. Eventually, they find alternate routes. If the area becomes overdeveloped, a shortage of employees could occur. Also, demographics may change; for example as a neighborhood ages, perhaps young employees grow up and move on and are not replaced, and the workforce slowly becomes depleted. But those are problems for another time and place. Right now you have to get busy. There is a lot of work to do to get your site prepped.

This vignette illustrates a few important points about site selection. Be realistic, work with a professional and arm yourself with facts. More importantly, don't be blinded by illusions. Take the time to find out if your area is business-friendly. The easiest way to do this is by talking with other business owners; they will let you know. If your location is out-of-the-way you might check with the city to ensure that there is no possibility of the area being seized by eminent domain for new development. Find out about fees, restrictions on signage, trash and waste removal, grease trap requirements and sewerage.

You want to ensure that you will have sufficient flow of

traffic. An important source for information on traffic flows is a regional or metropolitan planning organization if you have one in your area; also your state's Department of Transportation may be able to help. Of course the old-fashioned way to do this is to pick the key times of day and watch the traffic yourself to get an idea of the flow. Thirty years ago my father-in-law picked his first site by doing just that. He also defied some other long held and cherished conventions in choosing his first site. However, from that day to the day of this writing, that restaurant has continued to be one of our highest grossing. Finally, a good commercial real estate broker should be able to provide helpful information about traffic patterns and growth patterns for your area. In addition to traffic flow it is important that your customers be able to access your site. If there is a median, it may block access to traffic traveling in one direction. We have a restaurant with just such a dilemma, and we, along with other businesses on this strip, have petitioned the city repeatedly to remove that median, to no avail. If your guest cannot easily make that turn, he will continue on and go to the next food outlet that is accessible, so when choosing your site, keep this in mind.

Another important factor governing the success of any business is the socio-economic characteristics of an area. You will need to know the income per household, ethnic composition and population density in order to match your concept to your customer. One great place to start is the site for the U.S. Census Bureau at Factfinder.census.gov. There you will find scads of information on the demographics of your area. Your chamber of commerce will also have helpful information on your city's demographics.

Keep in mind the need for a stable workforce when choosing your location. If you don't have a stable workforce, then you will have to attract employees from other areas and this can be tricky; you may have to compensate them additionally for a commute that is greater than customary. Also, your workforce may need access to public transportation nearby.

While on the subject of different areas and demographics, I think it is important to remember that all demographics need food. For instance, some high risk or high crime areas do exist that have very successful food establishments. There is no reason to not locate in these areas as long as you are selling what the customer is buying. Remember: always match the concept with the audience and, always be culturally sensitive: don't bring a restaurant heavy on the pork offerings into a mainly Jewish or Muslim neighborhood—not a good idea. Just take a little time to get to know the area, and, if you can afford to, bring a well known person from that community on board your operation. Use common sense safety precautions in higher risk locations. By narrowing the field using the information above, you can pinpoint with better certainty the real cost of a location; you also greatly improve your chances of success.

When you have found a couple of sites that you think might be suitable for your new restaurant, then it is time to put the pencil to the paper and do some math to make sure things work out. You want to evaluate how different rents may affect your bottom line. You will need to be able to make reasonable estimates of both cash inflows and cash outflows. Consult your realtor, other restaurateurs and your CPA for sound estimates of these expenses. Here I present an analysis of two sites, that are near one another, for locating a franchise concept restaurant. How do the rents affect the bottom line and what can you live with?

Document # 1

	Site A		Site B	
Revenue	$ 80,000		$ 90,000	
Cost of goods	$ 25,600	32%	$ 28,800	32%
	$ 54,400	68%	$ 61,200	68%
Payroll	$ 19,200	24.00%	$ 21,600	24.00%
Payroll tax	$ 1,469	1.84%	$ 1,652	1.84%
Royalties	$ 4,000	5.00%	$ 4,500	5.00%
Ad royalty	$ 2,400	3.00%	$ 2,700	3.00%
Utilities	$ 3,500	4.38%	$ 4,500	5.00%
Uniforms	$ 800	1.00%	$ 1,000	1.11%
Linen	$ 1,300	1.63%	$ 1,700	1.89%
Accounting/Legal	$ 1,100	1.38%	$ 1,200	1.33%
Loan note payable	$ 3,500	4.38%	$ 4,200	4.67%
Restaurant supplies	$ 875	1.09%	$ 1,050	1.17%
Advertising	$ 2,000	2.50%	$ 2,000	2.22%
Maintenance	$ 1,098	1.37%	$ 1,500	1.67%
Insurance	$ 1,700	2.13%	$ 2,000	2.22%
Office supplies	$ 750	0.94%	$ 750	0.83%
Rent	$ 4,000	5.00%	$ 8,750	9.72%
Net income	$ 6,708	8%	$ 2,098	2%

Let's examine these two. Site B is bigger and has higher rent. After consulting professionals you decide it will have higher sales. In both cases we are above the breakeven threshold, and on the face of it, site A seems preferable. If there is no real defect for site A that puts it at a disadvantage when compared to site B, then the choice is simple. Sometimes a site may have a slight defect; maybe it is slightly less visible from the road, maybe to the backside of a mall, or set too far back on its lot and this could impact sales over the long term. You have to consider every angle when making such an important decision.

A special note regarding this pro-forma statement: the normal income statement does not include the principal portion of a note payable; only the interest is included. It's included here for cash flow purposes to determine whether we "break even" or not.

Many commercial leases are what are known as "Triple Net Lease." Under the terms of most triple nets, the tenant assumes most responsibility for the building including: taxes, insurance, maintenance, etc. Basically, if it breaks, you fix it. The only contact your landlord has with you is when you send him or her that rent check; unless, that is, maybe he or she drops a gift basket by for Christmas. If you decide to lease your building and you are doing a "build-out" make sure to negotiate a period of time for the build out before you actually start paying rent. In other words, state up front and have it stipulated in the lease that you would like 90 days or 120 days for construction or remodeling before you start paying rent. Only after that time has elapsed do you begin to pay rent. Not all landlords will be willing to do this, particularly in a hot real estate market, but it never hurts to ask. It is important that you discuss this with your contractor, get clear timelines and then negotiate sufficient time for the work to be completed. Don't underestimate. This way you don't start hemorrhaging cash right away. You got it? *NYCWG*!

So, let's summarize: pick a site with good traffic flow in an area that promises to grow for the foreseeable future. Make sure your site has easy ingress and egress and easy parking. Match your restaurant concept with your customer base and make sure you have adequate workforce nearby. Try to ascertain if any big infrastructure plans are on the books for your area; a major road job can put you out of business. And make sure that your area won't be the next "land-grab" through eminent domain. If you are building out, negotiate time for build-out before rent starts. You can't make right decisions until you know the total cost of your site, and to know that total cost there is some homework you must do.

One post script for this chapter: If you can afford it, the following is a scenario that may work well for you. Also, it may be a way to transfer wealth to your children. Set up a separate LLC or corporation for real estate holdings and buy your restaurant location through the corporation/LLC. Your standard 30-year fixed rate loan will run somewhere between 0.6 of 1% percent to 1% of the value of the loan give or take a little. So, for the sake of argument, let's make it 1%. If your loan amount is $350,000, your monthly note will be somewhere in the neighborhood of $3,500. Again, this is an approximation.

Typically, monthly rent should fall between 4% and 10% of net sales. You have projected to do $80,000 in sales per month at this location. Using 7% of that projected sales figure, your rent would be $5,600. Your restaurant makes that payment to your real estate holding company. You earn income with every rent payment, you build equity and your liability is reduced through the corporation/LLC. Also, this might be a great way to transfer wealth to your children if they are co-members or shareholders in this real estate LLC or corporation (check applicable laws in your state governing minor [below 18 years old] shareholders or minor membership in LLC's). Can you envision how that might work? Whereas, when you lease, once you write that check for rent, the money is gone; this way, each time you write your rent check, your wealth grows. Whether you lease or buy, you are still going to write a check every month, so why not let that money circle back to you? If you are just getting started it may be wise to lease, with an option to purchase, at first, to make sure that you actually do the sales you projected. Are you gettin' it? *NYCWG!* This example is for illustrative purposes only. With these, as well as any other financial matters in this book, I am not the final authority. It is important that you discuss these and any matters pertaining to business or finance with your attorney and CPA before making any decisions. My advice is not a substitute for legal advice.

Quickfax

- *The three C's: Congruency/Concept/Customer!*
- *Make sure you have sufficient customer base and that they will buy what you are selling.*
- *Make sure you have sufficient employee base.*
- *Make sure you have sufficient traffic and ease of entry and exit.*
- *Any big infrastructure plans on the books? Possible eminent domain?*
- *Don't automatically dismiss a less than desirable neighborhood. Just make sure you do your homework. Hire a well known local if you can.*
- *Negotiate time for build out into lease.*

- *Consider the option to purchase your site and pay yourself. Make sure to do it through a corporation or LLC for liability protection.*
- *NYCWG!*

Well, I've talked till I'm blue in the face and you haven't said a word. What do you think? Is it making sense; are things starting to gel? *NYCWG!* Now that we've talked about whether or not to franchise and we've dealt with the subject of locations a little, maybe it's time to turn our attention to the actual formation of a business. Turn the page.

Chapter 3

Getting Started

Cooking With Gas Mission Statement:

"To be your Prophet for Profit."

My mission is to help you stay in business. To do that you have to make at least some profit. Cooking with Gas does not suggest what type of restaurant business you should get into nor does it promise to make you millions by tomorrow like those shrill, garish commercials. Instead, it teaches you how to go about setting up a legal entity that will conduct business and assume certain liabilities in your stead; we then go a little further to help you with operations. If you set up your company correctly and have a good idea and sufficient capital to endure the vagaries of first-year business, then your business will flourish. Your business will provide you with livelihood commensurate with your effort, it will protect you and your personal assets in time, and it's fun! Cooking with Gas is a succinct look at the inner workings of business set-up and operation, with its main focus on the restaurant business. We cover many important topics relative to all businesses, but provide in-depth knowledge for restaurant operators in particular, such as food and labor costs, human resources, insurance and taxes, which most first time restaurateurs know little or nothing about. We finish out with a little lagniappe, food for thought, which are observations made from years in business that may be helpful to you. You may also visit our website at www.cookingwithgas.net for many important links, legal and accounting help, training materials and helpful knowledge about a variety of other topics. For your convenience we also offer consulting services at a low cost.

I love the restaurant business and would love to help you achieve your dreams, but know this: the work is hard. After reading this book, you may decide that opening a restaurant is more trouble than you thought. Let me assure you that this is correct. I am duty bound to first try and scare you away from your crazy dream. In fact, years ago there was a TV special called Scared Straight. That's what the subtitle of this book should be. It was a graphic look at the inner life of prison and its purpose was to scare a group of teenage boys into not doing certain things. Similarly, it is my goal to present, as honestly as possible, the difficulty ahead. Whether you do things wrong or do them right, this is most likely the most difficult and complex type of business you could choose. There is much work in front of you if you are thinking of opening a restaurant, and there will be many hoops for you to jump through. To run a business correctly is challenging, but a little effort and money spent doing it right increases your chances for success and is a heckuva lot cheaper than a business failure. If you are still reading, let's move on.

So you have a great idea and you are ready to get started. Well, let's talk. How much capital (money, assets) do you have and how much will you need to begin your business? If you are like most people, your resources are limited and you will need to borrow at least a portion of your start-up capital; in which case you will need to draw up a business plan.

A business plan is the road map you will provide to first get your ideas firm and then to interest possible investors. In it you will outline, in narrative form, your business idea—whether restaurant or courier service—fully describing your skills, your product or service, and your customer. This part of the business plan is called the executive summary. You will define your vision, which spells out the "Big Picture" as you see it. In the executive summary you need to convey the essence of your business to the reader in a thrilling and motivating way, while at the same time avoiding hyperbole. This can be a challenging task, particularly the first time out, but don't give up. If you have sources of capital such as a second mortgage or family loans, you would list those here. You will have to know who your competition is, what your location is and know something about the demographics of your chosen area. You will have to construct pro-forma financial statements, etc. This process forces you to answer difficult questions that you may not have thought of and to look earnestly and deeply into your idea. This is somewhat difficult, because when you get down and dirty, you may not like what you see; more importantly, your potential benefactor may not like what he or she sees. If your idea survives this stage, there may be hope, but you ain't there yet. A lender won't just hand you money. This first stage is critical. Make sure your ducks are in a row and that your credit is right. Your lender will furnish you with business plan formats but don't overlook another good resource, the Small Business Association. Also, visit our website at www.cookingwithgas.net for helpful tips and links to sites to assist you in creating your winning business plan. Do your own, informal business plan now by providing the following information:

Quickfax

- *What is your net worth?*
- *Construct your own executive summary. Exactly what is your business and how will you work within it?*
- *What form of business organization will you use?*
- *What are your abilities in the business of your choice? Your resume?*
- *What product or service do you provide?*
- *Market Analysis: Who is your competition? How good is your location? What are the demographics of your chosen area? What is the labor pool like for your type business in your area? (See chapter 2)*
- *Do pro-forma income statement, cash flow statements and balance sheet.*
- *How much do you need to borrow?*

By answering these questions, you get much closer to reality and can ask yourself: "Is my idea really feasible?" This is just a preliminary plan, but it gives you a pretty good idea whether or not your idea is pretty good! Remember that you and the bank have to come to an agreement. Ahem, let me rephrase that: They have to give you some money. The trouble is that borrowers and lenders have conflicting needs and wants. Typically we hear that while all borrowers need money, lenders only want to lend money to people who don't seem to need it. Sounds logical, but that is not altogether true. Banks make their living by lending and if they only loaned to no-risk clients, they would not lend much. The truth is they lend all the time to clients of varying degrees of risk. Often, though, it is true that greater risk costs more. The less credit-worthy you are, the more you will pay in interest on your debt, so build good credit and keep it that way. Remember: It's expensive to have poor credit!

Your prospective lender wants you to be confident and know exactly what it is you want to do, and a well-organized, good business plan and vision demonstrate that you do.

Previously, I mentioned having a Vision. An important part in the set-up of business is the creation of your *mission statement*. The mission statement condenses and focuses your vision. Your mission statement is the mold into which you pour your ideas. Stay true to it and your company will resemble it. The mission statement should be a brief, (one to five sentences) philosophical statement outlining the founder's core beliefs and values directly pertaining to his business and its operation. This one requires thought, and like the business plan, it forces you to understand what it is your company is all about; it's not done for you, but by you for the rest of the world. It should endure the passage of time gracefully and could outlive its author, so spend a little time and make it right. The mission statement usually addresses the customer. Rarer, but important in this author's opinion, is one that addresses both the customer and the employee (the external customer and the internal customer—more on that later). A well crafted mission statement is a thing of beauty. Examples of various mission statements are provided in the appendix and also online at www.cookingwithgas.net. Are you gettin' it? *Now You're Cooking With Gas! (NYCWG!)* Enough said on the subject.

Okay, you know what business you are going into, you have a vision and mission statement, you have done an informal business plan, and, by golly, things look pretty good. In that case, you should start getting excited now. Okay, that's long enough. Back to reality—we have a lot of wood left to chop. The business plan and vision/mission statement force your head down out of the clouds and into reality. If you still think your idea is good, then let's talk about organization.

Chapter 4

Business Organization Types

Would you venture into a really dangerous neighborhood unprotected? I know your answer already: you wouldn't. But if you are considering getting into the restaurant business, you are, trust me, entering a very dangerous neighborhood (figuratively speaking) fraught with many hidden perils. Remember Delila? Sure you do. That's why I ask again: do you venture into a bad neighborhood unprotected? Of course not. Obviously, if you had to go into a bad neighborhood, you would wrap yourself in some form of protection. Likewise, when entering the business world you should have protection too. And the protection you would shield yourself with is one of the following forms of business organization.

- Corporations: C corporations and sub-chapter S corporations
- Limited Liability Companies (LLC's)

This book is devoted to the entrepreneurial, small business start-up, with a focus on corporations and limited liability companies. There are other forms of business organization such as partnerships, limited liability partnerships, etc., which are most commonly used by legal and accounting firms, and there is plenty of information available on them at your library or online.

Some readers may understand what corporations and limited liability companies are, but a good number don't. If you are thinking of starting a business, or are already in business but are still operating as a sole proprietorship, you definitely need to read this book because you are unprotected and vulnerable in a very real sense. Here's why: the most common form of business organization is the sole proprietorship. It places you, the business owner, squarely in the crosshairs. When bad things happen, all liability flows directly to you. Should your business have financial difficulty and, say, go bankrupt, your personal assets, home, cars, jewelry, furniture, etc. may be attached. Your creditors could legally take everything you own. Yes, everything! If you believe this could or would never happen to you, stop reading this book right now and donate it to someone willing to learn. You already know everything. The rest of you who are a bit more realistic, take heed:

Your corporation or LLC will protect you. Let me explain: To the government you, dear reader, are a tax-paying entity with a unique identification number (your social security number). To state and federal taxing agencies that is all you are. You are able to conduct business, earn and spend money, build good credit—or go bankrupt. When things go wrong, all liability falls to you. You are responsible, and that responsibility will include releasing your assets to settle your liabilities.

When you set up a corporation or LLC, you "give birth" to a new tax-paying entity just like the one described above. It has its own identification number, the Employer Identification Number (EIN), and is really no different in the eyes of the law than a human being. This tax-paying entity is able to conduct business, earn and spend money, build good credit and, yes, go bankrupt. And when things go wrong in business, it falls to the LLC or corporation. That's it right there. Did you get it? Look a little closer. *When things go wrong, liability flows to the corporation or LLC.* This is what is commonly called "the corporate shield." Say your corporation owns Bob's Burger Barn and one of your waitresses drops a tray on a customer's head knocking her unconscious. If you're a sole proprietor, the customer can come after you and your personal assets, but if you conduct your business through a corporation, she may only attach the assets of the corporation. Lucky for you, there is a layer of separation. Your corporation stands between your creditors and your personal assets. There are two very important caveats to the corporate shield: first, in your corporation's or LLC's early life, you will be required to be its guarantor for loans, credit cards and trade accounts. It's like being a co-signer for a family member. During this phase you will be liable for whatever the terms of the particular liability is. In time, the LLC or corporation develops its own credit history, just like a person, and will stand alone. It is a fabulous feeling to create your own corporation or LLC and watch it grow. Second, if you yourself cause the injury or harm to the guest, even though you are incorporated, you may be held personally liable and that guest may come after your personal assets. Corporations, or my favorite, Limited Liability Companies (LLC's), are granted by the state you live in and there are some differences from state to state.

Forming your own corporation or LLC is very easy. An attorney created my first LLC. His fee was about $700, he took forever, and the guy never returned my calls for information when I wanted to know what was going on. My little deal just wasn't important enough for him to be bothered with. It was very frustrating and I had to pay big bucks for the privilege. However, at the time, forming an LLC was a great unknown to me, requiring magical skills possessed only by a highly paid attorney. Now I know that nothing could be further from the truth. Most states have made this process very easy, and, of course we at Cooking With Gas, LLC would be happy to assist. This is what you do: Go online to www.cookingwithgas.net for links to every secretary of state in all 50 states. It is through your secretary of state's office that you apply for your corporation or LLC. You'll also find a list of addresses and phone numbers. (This information is also printed in the appendix of this book.) So let's get started. What follows is an outline of business set-up. But first, keep in mind that if, at any stage you feel you need help, call us at 1—877—433—4664; we are here to help you.

It all begins with an idea. Whether you are starting from the ground up or purchasing a franchise, you will want to incorporate or form an LLC. You will also need to write your ideas out. At some stage you will have to put your ideas on paper, do a business plan and write vision/mission statement. And as you do these things, you will find that your business begins to take shape and come into focus. If you need additional financing, and most do, this is the stage to you secure it.

The next step begins to make your business concrete. When forming either a corporation or LLC, some states require you to conduct a name search to make sure that no one else has the name you want to use. Of course, the quickest way to do this is to have us do it for you, but you can call your secretary of state using the number provided by us, or log on to your secretary of state's web site using the links found on www.cookingwithgas. net . You should decide on a first choice of business name as well as a couple of alternates. For example, say you have selected Paul's Pizza, LLC as your primary name, but when you do your name search you find that it has already been taken. As a backup you might have Paul's Kitchen, LLC or Pizza Kitchen, LLC (Paul's Pizza Kitchen, LLC may not work because of its similarity to the name already taken). In most cases you will have a legal name by the time you are finished. Different states will hold your name for different periods. *NYCWG.*

After your name has been secured (some states will hold or "park" a name for a brief period), you will file for your corporation or LLC. For each state you will file an Articles of Organization and sometimes an initial report for an LLC, or Articles of Incorporation for a corporation and sometimes an initial report for a corporation. You will need to print this form, fill it out, and then fax or mail it with payment information to your secretary of state. Many states offer expedited assistance for additional fees.

One final note: often your secretary of state's website provides further information on other regulatory bodies with whom you may need to deal, such as the state Department of Revenue, Department of Labor, or other helpful information. Make sure you jot that information down for future reference.

Articles are similar for both types of organization. The required information is:

Corporation

Articles of Incorporation

The name of your company, which must always, thereafter be referred to with the designation of comma followed by Inc., Co.,Corp., Ltd. after your company name. For example: *Mother's Fried Chicken, Inc.*

Next they will want to know the duration of your business and, in most cases that is **Perpetual**, the thinking being that your business will go on forever.

Any lawful purposes for which you are organizing your business. For example, *"Mother's Fried Chicken, Inc.* is a small family diner featuring delicious southern fried chicken, side items and beverages." Or, *"Papa's Pies, LLC* manufactures an assortment of pastries which are sold to retail outlets such as grocery stores, convenience stores and gas stations for resale."

If a Corporation, the number of shares of common stock the corporation shall have the authority to issue.

If a Corporation, the names and signatures of all incorporators, the names of the first directors and the name of the registered agent at the business office. A street address is required.

Limited Liability Company (LLC)

Articles of Organization

The name of your company, which must always, thereafter be referred to with the designation comma followed by LLC after your company name. For example: *Papa's Pies, LLC.*

Next they will want to know the duration of your business and in most cases that is **Perpetual**, the thinking being that your business will go on forever.

Any lawful purposes for which you are organizing your business. For example, *"Mother's Fried Chicken, Inc.* is a small family diner featuring delicious southern fried chicken, side items and beverages." Or, *"Papa's Pies, LLC* manufactures an assortment of pastries which are sold to retail outlets such as grocery stores, convenience stores and gas stations for resale."

If an LLC, the names and addresses of the first members (owners) and managers, and the name of the registered agent at the business office. A street address is required.

With those forms, combined with filing fees, you can form a corporation or limited liability company today in every state in the union. As soon as you have Articles in your hot little hands, log onto the IRS website also found on www.cookingwithgas.net and apply for your Employer Identification Number (EIN) using IRS form SS-4. In most cases it will be issued instantly and, as always, we at Cooking With Gas, LLC are ready to assist. There you have it. In one, maybe two days, you have a legal business entity in the eyes of your state and the federal government and you didn't get scalped by a dang lawyer; I just saved you at least $500! You're welcome!

The EIN is just like a Social Security Number for your business. It is required in order for you to register with city, county and state taxing authorities, set up bank accounts, trade accounts etc. Now you may open a business banking account and trade accounts. Having your own Corporation or LLC is no guarantee of success, but it is a guaranteed way to protect yourself.

At the end of each year you will be required to pay an annual report fee to your state, which merely lets them know you are still in business and have the same officers. Also some states have what's called a franchise tax. Find these fees and other helpful info online at www.cookingwithgas.net. You must take the time to educate yourself and be informed of annual fees and taxes on corporations and LLC's in your state so you don't get caught unaware at the end of the year. Penalties for late payment of these fees can be stiff.

Just one more note before we move on. If you form a corporation, consider forming a sub chapter-s corp. The sub-s is not subjected to the same double taxation (corporate and then shareholder) as a regular c-corporation. Typically c-corporations are larger entities comprised of hundreds of shareholders. The s-corporation is a designation granted by the IRS for special tax treatment. An eligible domestic corporation can avoid double taxation (once to the corporation and again to the shareholders) by electing to be treated as an s-corporation. Generally, an s-corporation is exempt from federal income tax other than tax on certain capital gains and passive income. On their tax returns, the s-corporation's shareholders include their share of the corporation's separately stated items of income, deduction, loss, and credit, and their share of non-separately stated income or loss.

I said earlier that I preferred the LLC. Here are some of the reasons. A corporation must have a chairman and a board of directors, hold meetings and keep records of those meetings (called minutes) recorded by the secretary. Feasibly, a corporation might have a single shareholder who acts in all of the above capacities (conduct meetings while acting as chairman, board, secretary, etc.), but that seems a little silly, especially in light of the fact that the LLC offers so much in the way of favorable tax treatment and protection of your personal assets all without those onerous meeting and record keeping requirements. Do some research to discover which form of organization you would be most comfortable with. In addition, if you have any questions of a legal nature, you should consult your attorney as the information provided herein, while sound, is not to be construed as a substitute for legal advice. Does this make sense to you? Are you starting to get it? *NYCWG!*

So, again you ask, "why do I need to do this? Why not just remain a sole proprietor?" Well, in addition to the reasons stated above, many sole proprietors often don't keep good books and don't manage cash flow and financial statements correctly. Items that may have been an expense to a company, thereby reducing net income and resulting taxes, are items that sole proprietors often miss. Also, depreciation on equipment is a huge non-cash expense that reduces taxable income. At the end of the year Willie, of *Willie's Lawn Service,* dutifully claimed all his income, but failed to take the depreciation for the four large mowers, several edgers, blowers, etc. that he purchased during the year.

That depreciation would have reduced his taxable income substantially. It is the same with your equipment, computers, furnishings, improvements, etc. Most Americans are honest about their earnings but turn around and leave money on the table when it comes to deductions mainly through ignorance. When you organize a business as a corporation or LLC, you will set up accounting software and begin accounts receivable (monies owed to you), and accounts payable (monies you owe) and other general journal accounts. You will capitalize all your "big ticket" items on the books (in your accounting software—ask your CPA how this is done). At the end of the year you bring all this information to your CPA for tax purposes. Transactions in these accounts, combined with cash transactions are transferred over to your balance sheet, income statements, statement of cash flows and finally the retained earning statement.

The balance sheet is so called for the equality or "balance" between assets and liabilities. The income statement (sometimes called profit and loss or simply P & L) takes net revenues and deducts operating and administrative expenses from those revenues to end up with net income. This is the statement you will need to become most intimately familiar with; in the restaurant business you live by it. One more statement you should be familiar with is the cash flow statement, 'cause if you ain't got cash, nothing else really matters. The cash flow statement takes beginning cash for the period and adds to it all cash received during the period (from sales and financing activities such as the sale of stock) to arrive at total cash available and then subtracts all cash disbursements, with the resulting sum or difference being this period's ending and next period's beginning cash balance. All small business accounting software puts these statements together for you. The income statement is where we see the results of operations and whether you are actually making money or not. As you become more familiar with the income statement, it offers greater and greater opportunities. So let's crack the seal.

Quickfax: The Organization Set-up Process
- *All businesses begin as an idea.*

- *Refine your idea by writing it out. This stage may include a business plan.*
- *Secure needed financing.*
- *Log on to your secretary of state's website using www. cookingwithgas.net and do a name search to see if the name you have selected for your corporation or LLC has been taken.*
- *Log on to your secretary of state's website and print forms for registering as a corporation or LLC. In most cases the fees may be paid by credit card, which speeds up the process (some states offer expedited assistance for an additional fee). Fax or mail forms and payment.*
- *When you receive your certificate from your secretary of state, log on to IRS.gov and file for your Employer Identification Number.*

Now that you have your business set up, you may want to consider doing the following:

- *Open your business checking account with your bank (EIN required).*
- *Register with local regulatory bodies such as fire, plumbing, electrical, city and county tax collection departments, and with your state's Department of Revenue for tax collection and remittance. At every stage ask questions to ensure that you cover every contingency.*
- *If you will be purchasing equipment, inventories or supplies of any kind begin contacting vendors. In most cases you will need to fill out a credit application so start the process early.*
- *Maybe now you can see how some form of business organization would have protected Delila.*
- *NYCWG!*

Chapter 5

Financial Statements

What's your net worth? How much did your business profit last year? What is profit? And is it really important? What?! You mean you can't answer some of these questions? Well, you're not alone, so don't feel bad. Most Americans don't know their net worth or that profit ain't always all it's cracked up to be (think taxes). Chapter 5 provides a quick overview of what the basic financial statements are with a brief description of the balance sheet, income statement and the statement of cash flows.

The financial statements tell you what you own (assets), the claims against what you own (liabilities) and what you have profited (net income) for a certain period.

There are four financial statements. They are:
- The Balance Sheet
- The Income Statement
- The Cash Flow Statement
- Retained Earnings Statement

We will focus mainly on the balance sheet, income statement and cash flow statement, but if you are serious, you will need to develop a working understanding of all these statements and how they work together. These four parts make a whole that tells the story of how your business is doing.

The Balance Sheet

The balance sheet is so named because it shows the

"balance" or equality between assets and liabilities at a point in time, but, like everything it's not quite that simple. It's actually Assets = Liabilities + Owner's Equity. Let me elucidate.

Say your house (asset) is valued at $200,000, has claims against it (liability) of $125,000 and a certain portion that you own (owner's equity) of $75,000.

$200,000 = $125,000 + $75,000

Assets	Liabilities + Owner's Equity
$200,000	$125,000
	$ 75,000

There, that's a balance sheet! They get a lot bigger and badder than that, but that is the essence of a balance sheet—a financial snapshot of a brief moment in time. You can see that it's only for today because soon you will make another payment and your equity will increase and the liability will decrease. Also, there are factors that affect the value of your asset, such as the appreciation of property values. Calculate the effect on owners equity above if property value increases by $25,000 in one year. For a business balance sheet, all things owned by the business (cash, stocks, property, plant, equipment & inventory) are listed to the left of the equal sign and all claims against assets on the right. You then plug the difference into owner equity. The balance sheet, in conjunction with income statement, gives decision makers like management, owners, and lenders an idea of a company's or individual's financial well-being. So, there it is—a snapshot in time of your business. That's what the balance sheet is.

Next, let's look into the income statement, also referred to as the profit and loss, or simply P & L statement. Even with me trying to simplify financial statements, they are, at first, a little complex, so pay close attention here, because the income statement is very important to your success.

The Income Statement

In a nutshell, the income statement lists all revenues from sales or services less all expenses related to those sales or services. What is left is called "net income" and when you are organized as a sub-s corporation or LLC, the net income of your company (after depreciation) is added to your personal taxable income. Let's use *Gert's Gumbo Shop, LLC* as an example. (Note: the parentheses below indicate that you subtract that number.)

Revenue from sales:	$ 1,000
Expenses:	$ (806)
Income:	$ 194

This is a simplified example and we will expand on this form momentarily. Just a little aside and then we'll move on. You have no doubt heard the expression *"The Bottom Line."* Well, that's it right there. Net income after taxes is the bottom line. I just wanted to tell you that in case you didn't already know it. Anyhow, back to the subject at hand. In most retail businesses—and the restaurant business is no different—the first expense listed is the primary item sold and it is a separate line item called "cost of goods sold." If we use a restaurant as an example, it would be the cost of food used during the period. Cost of goods is calculated by adding to beginning inventory all goods purchased during the period and then subtracting out the ending inventory. (Beginning inventory + purchases −ending Inventory = cost of goods sold). Cost of goods is deducted from revenue leaving a new number called gross profit (not to be confused with profit, which is what most people call net income) Also, the dollars on the income statement are expressed as a percentage of revenue.

Revenue from sales:	$	1,000	100%
Cost of goods sold:	$	(320)	32%
Gross profit:	$	680	68%
Expenses:	$	(486)	49%
Net income:	$	194	19%

In the above example we focused our microscope a little, and we are beginning to see more, but this example is still simplified. There is a little more expansion required to bring this creature called the income statement into focus. In this example there was a line item called expenses. On all income statements expenses are detailed, and in our business it always begins with our second greatest, most important and controllable expense. Those of you who have been, or are in the food business now, know that I am talking about labor, or payroll expense. The cost of food, typically called food cost, and labor, typically called labor or payroll, are your greatest expenses and present the greatest challenges to control. Always remember the following:

Quickfax

- *Net income is a function of expense control. Save a dollar on labor or food while keeping sales the same and that dollar flows down to income.*

Those who have started restaurants without previous experience have learned these lessons the painful way. Now I want to expand on that expense line for Gert's Gumbo Shop.

Revenue from Sales:	$ 1,000	100%
Cost of Goods Sold:	$ (320)	32%
Gross Profit:	$ 680	68%
Expenses:		
Payroll expense:	$ (250)	25%
Payroll taxes:	$ (19)	2%
Rent:	$ (50)	5%
Utilities:	$ (45)	5%
Insurance:	$ (25)	3%
Interest on debt:	$ (15)	2%
Restaurant supplies:	$ (25)	3%
Office supplies:	$ (20)	2%
Maintenance expense:	$ (37)	4%
Net income:	$ 194	19%

That's an income statement, and by the way, Gert's Gumbo Shop is doing well. A 19.39% net income is a respectable return. For larger companies, expenses are sorted by those derived from operations, called operating expenses, and those that go to administering, called administrative expenses. Operating expenses are just like the ones you see in the example above; those expenses directly related to operations. Administrative expenses are salaries of office personnel and executives, insurance, and overhead required to run a business.

The business year can be divided into twelve calendar months or into thirteen 28—day periods. At the end of each business period you will prepare your own in-house P&L, and, if your business can afford it, you forward all financial information to your CPA. He or she will compile your financials, including the balance sheet and income statement, and will assist you in analyzing the information to improve efficiencies where possible. At the end of the year, you will bring all of your financial information to your CPA for tax preparation. To keep your accounting expenses down, be as organized as you possibly can. Keep good records and provide clear, uncluttered data. Now maybe you are beginning to see some of the ways an organized business can be your best friend. Now you're Cooking with Gas! *NYCWG!*

Listed here are some benefits of owning your own business that can also save you money. Consult your CPA for more ideas.

- Put yourself on salary.
- Put your kids on salary for any task around the business. A great way to transfer wealth. Consult your CPA.
- Lease your car through the business.
- Provide health and life insurance for family.
- Write off the portion of your home used as office space.
- Set up of pension plans.
- Set up of health savings accounts.
- Pay for internet services.
- Pay for cell phone.
- Club membership dues

There is plenty of room for creativity with business ownership. A great source of information on this subject is other business owners. Read every thing you can on the subject and talk with other business owners, your CPA and attorneys to further your understanding.

The Cash Flow Statement

The cash flow statement takes the ending cash from the previous period, which becomes beginning cash for this period, and adds to it all cash received during the current period (from sales and financing activities such as the sale of stock) to arrive at what is known as total available cash. All cash disbursements are then subtracted from total cash available, with the resulting sum or difference being your ending cash for this period and beginning cash for next period.

Beginning cash:	$ 1,200
Cash from operations:	$ 8,000
Total cash available:	$ 9,200
Cash disbursements	$ (7,300)
Ending cash balance	$ 1,900

The $1,900 ending cash position is forwarded to next period as beginning cash. For large corporations with various kinds of secondary income such as sales of stocks and bonds and large depreciations, the cash flow statement is a little more complex; for you and me it's going to look pretty much like this example.

You will need accounting software and there are many to choose from. They are easily found at the nearest office supplies store or may be purchased online at www.cookingwithgas. net. Some of the more popular brands are Great Plains, Quickbooks and Peachtree. They are all good and we make no recommendation.   There are two ways to account for your finances in business: they are called *accrual basis* and *cash basis* of accounting. When you set up your financial software, you will go through an interview process and this is one of the questions you will need to answer, so let me explain the difference.

Accrual Basis: Revenue is recorded in the books when the sale is made regardless of whether you received any cash or not. Expense is recorded when you received that good or service regardless of whether you spent cash or not.

Cash Basis: Revenue is recorded when you receive cash and expenses are recorded when you spend cash.

Cash basis works better for small businesses and many restaurateurs prefer this method. The accrual method is a little more complex and is better for businesses that are bigger and that create receivables; however I prefer the accrual method nonetheless. The thing to remember about accrual basis is that all revenues are not cash; likewise all net income is not cash. Under the accrual basis you might have $10,000 in receivables (an asset), which has lead to a healthy profit. (Never confuse profit for cash in the bank, a common mistake). Later you discover that those receivables are worthless. While receivables are an asset and do affect the income statement the same as cash, they are not cash and you can't buy groceries or pay bills with a receivable. We in the restaurant business do not typically have receivables, and unless you plan to allow charge accounts, you won't have them either, but I did want to make you aware. You should be aware of your cash position on a daily basis, and nothing but a well maintained checking account register will tell you that. Always be fanatical about keeping your checking register up to date. If your bank offers online banking, check your account daily to verify the deposits actually made into your account.

Quickfax

- *What is your net worth?*
  It is the sum of ALL your assets (real estate, stocks, bonds, cars, savings, checking, pensions, 401-k, business, jewelry, etc.) less your liabilities.
- *NYCWG!*

So let's say your assets total $500,000 and your liabilities $275,000. You do the math. That's right: $225,000 is your net worth. With today's ready credit, it is not at all unheard of to have a negative net worth. Let's try the same numbers as above, but let's rearrange them a little. Assets equal $275,000 and liabilities equal $500,000. Now you have a negative net worth of ($225,000); the more upside down you get, the greater risk you represent. The greater risk you are, the more your debt will cost you and, eventually, lenders will stop granting you credit. And always remember that it is very expensive to have poor credit. Net worth is the same thing as owner's equity.

One thing to always bear in mind is that assets change in value according to market conditions. In a hot real estate market your house could appreciate in value significantly in a short period of time thereby increasing your net worth significantly, as in the example above. Conversely, the stock market can turn south and, if you have a significant position, that would also affect your net worth. Keep a diversified mix of assets and always be aware of market trends and directions to maximize your net worth. I track my net worth monthly with a simple Excel spreadsheet. And I recommend the same for you. We have one if you're interested at www.cookingwithgas.net.

One more time:

Balance Sheet	**Income Statement**		**Cash Flows**
Assets = Liabilities + Owner's Equity	Revenue:	xxx	Beginning cash +
xxx | xxx	Expense:	(xx)	Cash from operations
xxx	Net income:	xx	Total cash available -
			(Cash disbursement)
			New cash position

Okay, you have your business set up and you know how you will account for your finances; let's talk about management.

Chapter 6

Management: Part one Planning and Controlling

Management

Okay, break out a box of #2's and keep the sharpener close, roll up your sleeves and brace yourself, 'cause I'm getting ready to put you to work. Make you think, that is. Delila gave us a lot to think about. The first five chapters dealt with administrative efforts that you need to perform in order to set up your business in preparation for operations. Now we get to the meat of the matter. This and the following few chapters address the subject of actual day-to-day operations.

There are four basic functions of management. They are:

- **Planning**
- **Controlling**
- **Organizing**
- **Influencing (Leading)**

Sear these into your grey matter.

Cooking with Gas is now going to give you a four year college degree's worth of business learnin' and save you a whole bunch of money; that is, unless you've already gone to college, in which case, too bad. You'll probably learn more here and it will cost a lot less. Any discussion of management also includes such topics as internal control, staffing and training, motivation and team building, and morale, and in the end each of these fall under one of the functions listed above.

What follows is an introduction to the functions of management, their purpose and implementation. The current chapter will handle planning and controlling and the next chapter will deal with organizing and influencing.

As stated above, management has four functions. Good management doesn't just happen by accident. It is a purposeful action. Management is defined as "Coordination of company resources (personnel, money and equipment) to achieve the stated mission and goals of the company." This is all done through the process of planning, organizing, influencing and controlling.

"If you fail to plan, you plan to fail."

Planning: The first and most important of all of the functions. In fact all others are subheadings of this most important of functions. You can't Organize, Control, or Influence without planning, so its importance to everything you do is easy to see. To plan, first ask yourself what your goal is, and then determine, **in advance**, what steps you will take to realize that goal. Plans should be specific and they should then be written down. Your plans should provide clear guidance for managers and employees.

Organizing: Is the process of dividing up the work to be done then assigning the correct person and resources to accomplish the company's goals. In other words, put your "aces" in their places and give them the proper tools to get the job done. This important function also includes "staffing." Staffing correctly is the single most important factor in determining a manager's success.

Influencing: This very important topic involves the leadership of others. It is the process of determining the behavior of another human being. A manager must accomplish company objectives through the efforts of others. As you cannot lead by shoving, the trick becomes to get the other to want to put forth the effort in pursuit of company objectives. This is the definition of Motivation. The best leaders learn what motivates individuals and then use this knowledge to direct their activities.

Controlling: Once the objectives and standards are set through planning, controlling is the process whereby we monitor performance and compare actual results against preset standards and take corrective action when necessary. Some examples of this are administrative paperwork, variance reports sometimes called perfect reports in the restaurant business, employee evaluations, etc.

Part I: Planning and Controlling

It all starts with planning, so that's where we'll start. You can't do anything in life without at least a little planning (certainly a little planning would have helped Delila). However, the more planning you do, the better organized your life will be; nothing is better for time management. In the restaurant business we plan constantly. Things like yields and projections, labor matrices and schedules are all tools we use in the planning process. We are always looking to the future and trying to reasonably predict it in order to have all the right resources in the right mix and on time to meet those future needs. Seat-of-the-pants is no way to fly. Gotta get scientific. So let's do it.

The greatest tool for planning in the restaurant business is projections. Projections are simply an average, usually of several past periods. I have always used the most recent four weeks. By doing so I capture the slower part of the month where people are lower on cash (although that matters less now that most quick service restaurants accept credit cards) and the busier part where they are a little more flush with cash. Let's start with an exercise: calculating the average for each day. To calculate an average, you add the column and then divide by the number of occurrences:

	Monday	Tuesday	Wednesday	Thursday	Friday	Saturday	Sunday
Week #1	$ 1,600	$ 1,920	$ 2,304	$ 3,226	$ 4,516	$ 4,064	$ 2,845
Week #2	$ 1,800	$ 2,125	$ 2,500	$ 3,250	$ 4,710	$ 4,211	$ 3,022
Week #3	$ 1,900	$ 2,321	$ 2,610	$ 3,526	$ 4,816	$ 4,378	$ 3,145
Week #4	$ 1,700	$ 2,018	$ 2,399	$ 3,326	$ 4,675	$ 4,150	$ 2,935

Let's start with Monday. The average for the past four Mondays is $1,750. That is the *projected* sales that I can reasonably expect to do this coming Monday based on historical data. Are you still with me? We will probably do right at $1,750 on Monday and now I have a solid number that I can plan with. So without further ado I'm gonna drop a new term on you. The term is **yield** and we use it in two different ways in our business:

- **Product yield** denotes the number of portions we get from a case or unit of something; for example a bag of mashed potato mix will yield 50 small servings, a bag of buffalo wings will yield 16 five-piece portions or a roll of hamburger meat will yield 40 quarter pound burger patties, but more important for our purposes here is the sales yield.

- **Sales yield** denotes the sales, in dollars, each time a unit of product moves out of your restaurant. Today we did $1000 in sales and we used four rolls of hamburger meat. What was our sales yield? Simple, just divide $1000 by 4, which equals $250. Okay, so this tells me that every time I took in $250, one roll of hamburger meat was used. Looking forward to Monday, I see that I am projected to do $1750 in sales, and I know that each time I do $250 in sales I'm going to use one roll of meat. That means I will need at least seven rolls of meat for Monday's business. Okay, so if a case of burger meat has eight rolls, tell me what I will need each day this week and a total for the week, but this time tell me in cases. You get it; now you're **planning** and *NYCWG*! That's really it. You can calculate yields on anything product, labor hours, whatever, and in any portion you decide. Typically you do it in the case unit for ordering purposes. For the sake of conversation let's say Delila actually knew what she was doing and had prepared a pro-forma income statement, which is nothing more than educated guesswork, and calculated week one's sales to be $35,000. Using available information, and realizing that McDonald's and Burrito Mundo were going to impact the movement of hamburger meat, she calculated the following yields:

Beef Spareribs Yield: $300 per case

Rib Eye Steaks: Yield: $125 per pack; 4 packs per case

Hamburger Meat: $45,000 per case

How many cases of each did she need to have available for her projected sales?

Did you notice that very high yield on hamburger meat? Why was that? Let me explain: Recall that we defined yield as the dollars in sales each time a unit of product goes out of the restaurant. So if I do $3,000 in sales today and I used 12 rolls of meat, my yield is $250 per roll. Let's call a $250 yield "normal." Now take the same sales but this time using eight rolls of meat for the day's sales. Yield equals $375. Again, the same $3,000 in sales, but this time four rolls of meat were used, with yield equaling $750. Do you see that sales yield sky-rocketing? Finally $3,000 in sales but using only one roll of meat. My yield is $3,000. Wow! You see, as meat changes in my overall **sales mix** of items sold, its yield changes. Sales yields are inversely proportional to amount of product used. As above, the smaller a product's part of the mix becomes, the larger its sales yield becomes. The converse holds true as well: the larger a product's part of the sales mix is, the smaller its yield becomes. This is truly helpful knowledge.

Recall Delila's dilemma with hamburger meat. She had not adequately anticipated competition, and, as a result, hamburger meat was a very small percent of her sales mix. Let's say her sales for a week were $35,000 and she used 6.22 rolls of hamburger meat; her yield is a whopping $5,627 per roll of meat (remember, $250 is about normal for this example). At this rate, her yield is $45,000 per case when it should be $2,000 per case! See the worksheets at www.cookingwithgas.net for more practice on this very important concept.

In our businesses we use the yield for every order, and each order is designed to carry us through the day after the following delivery day. This sounds confusing, I know, but let me shed some light on it.

Order days and delivery days are Monday, Wednesday and Friday. Monday you place your order to be delivered on Wednesday, on Wednesday you place an order to be delivered Friday and finally, on Friday you place an order to be delivered Monday. Clear as mud? Great.

Let's say it's Monday and I am placing an order to be delivered on Wednesday. That order will need to carry me at least until my next delivery day, Friday, but since this ain't my first rodeo, I know that things happen: trucks break down, orders get shorted some key items, etc. so I always add a buffer of at least a half day's sales. If the sign out front says Bud's Burgers, I surely can't afford to run out of hamburger meat, but at the same time I don't want to carry too much inventory. Using yields will help to reduce product overage or underage and will also reduce waste.

There is a yield on human labor called productivity that greatly assists scheduling, and we will discuss that in an upcoming chapter. Can you see how this knowledge would've helped Delila? *NYCWG!* If she'd only been able to read this book before getting started!

We provide yield and productivity worksheets online at www.cookingwithgas.net, as well as very helpful spreadsheets for projecting and tracking sales and payroll costs, product usage, food costs and for our next important subject:

The Control Function

So why do we do all this? Remember Delila? Remember how

she was paying out so much on employees and food and yet she was still out of key items such as rib-eye steaks? The nice word for this phenomenon is "shrinkage." In truth it's called theft. Employee theft is your number one form of loss and it comes in a couple of different forms. One is non-productive time, what we in the business call "riding the clock." An employee is on the clock but not performing duties. He may be sleeping in the stockroom, listening to the radio out in his car or just staying in the restroom too long. These things add up to whopping sums of money and can sink you quickly. Another common form of loss is theft of food, and this also takes many different forms from the innocuous constant picking throughout the day to the serious crime of whole cases of very expensive rib-eye steaks going out of the back door concealed in a garbage can, or worse, just plain carried out by a trusted employee who feels he deserves it. All of these things and more were happening to Delila and she never knew it.

The control function combined with firm management will stop this problem. Remember, the control function is where you take a preset standard for performance and then compare your actual performance. Where actual performance differs, you take corrective action.

Back to Delila. She sold rib-eye steaks. She had no pre-set standard, but if she had, it would have looked something like this: "For every pack of rib-eyes I sell, I know that I will have a small percentage of waste. So let's just say that every time I sell one pack of rib-eyes, I also allow a factor of 5% additional for waste, such as fat that had to be trimmed away, or the occasional dropped steak." Her preset standard for the sale of one pack of rib-eyes is 1.05. That's one for the pack she is selling plus the factor of 5% for allowed waste.

At the end of her first week she had sold 60 cases (remember, there are four packs per case) so that would be 240 packs; 240 times her standard (240 x 1.05) equals 252 packs. So, by the end of the week, under perfect circumstances, her standard for sales of 240 packs is 252; that means she is "allowing" 12 packs as waste. However, upon completion of her inventory on Sunday night, she determines that she used 254 packs. She now calculates her **variance**: $254 - 252 = 2$, which means two additional packs over her standard were used. She will want to investigate why two additional packs were used.

In our business this is a very helpful tool that lets us know how efficiently we are performing. Right away the controlling function will indicate if there is a problem. In the Delila story, she had no idea where or what was happening with her food because she did no tracking at all. If she had been using a variance report and discovered that for the same 60 cases her variance was +20 packs, Delila would have known for a fact that she had a serious shrinkage problem and would probably have at least some idea of where to look. It isn't necessary that you do a variance on every item in your inventory. In fact, chances are that you have 10 inventory items or less that make up the majority of your food cost. Do a weekly variance report on those items. And remember, you know who to call if you need help.

Without tight internal control, it is doubtful you will succeed. You must have a handle on the movement and flow of all things through your restaurant, but specifically you want controls on food. You want controls on labor. You want controls on cash. If you don't maintain those controls, how can you truly know what your business is doing? We can help you set up systems for just such controls. Just log on to www.cookingwithgas.net. We talk further about standards for employees in the next chapter and really explore food and labor costs in the chapter titled "The Bully Twins."

Chapter 7

Management: Part two Organizing and Influencing

Part 2: Organizing and Influencing

Good help is so hard to find. I hear this complaint everywhere. All employers say it. It's blared from the tops of roofs and splashed across the front pages of national newspapers. It is truly a national crisis! God help us! You just can't find good help anymore. Period.

Well, that just ain't true. The world is full of great people. You've gotta know how to find them. I always shake my head and chuckle when I hear that lament, then I take issue—but don't let me get sidetracked.

While all topics are important, the staffing function is the most critical to your success. No coach will ever win games unless he gets the right players on the team and then trains them correctly. If you don't do this one correctly, you've shot a hole in the bottom of your boat before you've even left the dock.

First let's talk about you. What is your role in the scheme of things? Chew on this and then tell me what you think. You are the conductor of the orchestra, you know, the guy who looks like he's doing nothing at all but waving that silly little stick. He looks about as useful as a bump on a log. What the hell do they need him for anyway? I will tell you. Let him step down off that podium mid-song, and you will hear a train wreck. It is through him that the beautiful music happens; he is the one that all eyes look to for leadership; he is the keeper of the tempo; while it is a team of musicians that make the music, it is the guy with the baton that leads them. They get the job done together. In the restaurant business, you are that conductor. Make that what you do best; if the conductor isn't happy with his or her violinist and climbs down off the podium to take over that position, what happens? Train wreck. Same thing in our business: you get the work done through employees. If you allow yourself to be dragged into one position or another, all other areas suffer, and the music ain't as pretty. Some will say you don't look like you are doing anything and you might even feel that way from time to time, particularly if you have done the following things correctly and have created a winning team. A great staff makes your job so easy and fun that they make you look good.

Staffing[1] is defined as "having the right quantity and quality of employees in the right place, at the right time, to perform successfully the work of the company." Unfortunately we often approach this most important of functions far too casually and with too little forethought and planning. For example, when purchasing a saw or a car, we consider what our need is from that object and how we will use it, and then we select the item that most closely fits those needs. And yet we will turn around and hire someone on a whim with no consideration of the fit of that person to the specific requirements of the job. Remember Delila? Unfortunately, this style of hiring leads to low morale and high turnover, which has very high costs for any company.

The costs of staffing are not as easy to calculate as direct costs such as materials (food), but are nonetheless very high. For instance, the time a manager spends to interview, complete the new hire paperwork, orient and train a new employee costs **big** money because, while that manager is doing that, he or she is taken away from some other duty which must then be covered by another manager. In addition, while the employee is learning, he or she is less productive and wastes more, which also cost big money. Finally, as so often happens, the wrong person is selected in the first place and is non-productive from the start, which is not only costly, but also getting rid of that employee can sometimes be very difficult. These are just some of the hidden costs of the staffing function, so maybe now you can see how important this function is.

Staffing is a system made up of several key components:

- **Job analysis** — Basically this means defining the job duties and then determining the skills required to perform those duties.
- **Human Resource Planning** — Anticipate your future needs for employees.
- **Recruiting** —To attract qualified applicants.
- **Selection** — Choosing the employee that possesses the skills required to perform the tasks defined in job analysis or definition.
- **Training** — Once that person is selected, he or she is trained using the OJT or "three-step" method.
- **Performance Appraisal** — Evaluate performance and progress on the job.
- **Human Resource Administration** — Perform various staffing related internal functions.

Each of these can be understood alone, but together they work as an integrated system. They flow from one to the next and work together as a whole. Let's start at the top.

Job Analysis —What does it really mean? What it does is force you to define the job and exactly what the job requirements are and the type of candidate that would be most suitable for that position. This allows you to weed out unlikely candidates and to ask more pertinent questions of those that you do interview to determine if they possess the skills required.

Human Resource Planning —This type of planning answers the questions, "What will our employee needs be tomorrow? What will they be next week?" After job analysis, we determine employee needs according to projected business, upcoming specials, etc. Perhaps there will be a slowdown during the back-to-school time frame, or business will be picking up for the Christmas holidays. The important point is that you determine your needs ahead of time and **plan** accordingly, considering time for such things as interviewing, paperwork, training, etc.

Do not respond to needs after they occur, because by then it is far too late.

Recruiting —This is the process of attracting qualified applicants. How do we do this? One of the best resources for new employees is your current staff. Ask them if they have any friends who would like a job. Another method is to talk to people you meet who work in other restaurants, grocery stores or convenience stores. See if they are currently happy, though be careful here. Owners and managers guard their good employees carefully and may get upset with you for trying to "steal" their good employee. There are no laws against this type of poaching, but you will develop a bad reputation quickly if you pursue it. The best approach is the indirect approach. As you give that person your card, suggest that you have observed their great performance and ask that, if they have any highly motivated friends like themselves, they contact you. You can find some dynamite help this way. Other methods are handouts, flyers posted on message boards at high schools and colleges near your business, and newspaper classifieds. The key here is that recruiting requires activity on your part rather than waiting for that perfect applicant to walk through your door. We all know those are few and far between.

Selection —Selection is possibly the most critical part in the process. For that reason a little more time will be spent here. As stated above, selection is choosing the employee that fits the job requirements. You wouldn't put a 95-pound weakling in a job that required heavy lifting back in the warehouse, nor a blue collar laborer in the front office answering phones and typing memos. How do we determine if someone fits our job requirements? What do we look for? This is the important key that we sometimes forget and as a result we stumble through the interview process and send strong indications to the interviewee that we don't know what we are doing. He or she may exploit that later.

Let's start at the top. Chances are good that no one has set you down and taught you how to conduct an interview. What does it mean to be a good interviewer? It means you possess the knowledge and skill necessary. Knowledge and skill are learned traits. You are not just born with them. A good interviewer must first be at ease and then put his or her applicant at ease. He or she must have a sound knowledge of the company and the various workstations in the business and how they relate to one another. During the interview you must ask open-ended questions that require more than a yes or no answer, and then listen to the response. Be alert for key words and phrases that may shed light on the prospect's real attitudes, and whether he or she has the traits we look for in new hires. This is a skill that comes with education and experience, but let me get you headed in that direction.

Often when I interview, I like to ask questions about the interviewee's experiences, his or her likes and dislikes. I also ask what past or present employers would tell me about their punctuality, attitude, and behavior with superiors and I try to approach these topics from an oblique angle. For example:

Me: *"I see here on your application, Jaun, that your current employer is Jonnie Jumpup; this afternoon, when Jonnie Jumpup and I are talking, will he tell me that everything is good with you except that maybe you had a little problem getting to work on time?"*

Applicant: Tells you that he was always on time; in fact, he was even early most of the time. He looks you in the eye and appears honest; that's good. Or, he may let slip that he was occasionally late but it was no big deal. That's not good. That's your first red flag.

Me: "Okay, so Jonnie Jumpup and I are still talking and he tells me "everything was great with Jaun, he was always on time—that is, when he came to work. Trouble is that he has a lot of personal problems and as result has missed many days."

Applicant: *"No, he could never say that. I haven't missed one day since I started that job two years ago."* Again applicant is direct and sounds compelling. Again, that's a good sign. Or, he might confess that he has missed more days than he should, but that he now has those problems taken care of. Another red flag.

Me: "Okay, Jonnie Jumpup and I are just about done talking. Jonnie tells me: "no, everything was pretty good with Jaun, he was always on time, never missed a day, I just had this one little problem with Jaun: he seemed to resent authority. Anytime I, or one of my fellow managers, would ask him to do something, we would get a lot of resistance.

Applicant: Here your applicant asserts that he always got along with management, and again he communicates it well. Again, that's good. Or, maybe he suggests that he did have a problem or two, but it was always their fault because they didn't respect him. Let me translate that one for you—"No." Do not hire this person. This person has a problem with authority figures, and, if you hire him, you will have nothing but trouble. That's a big negatory ghost rider. Do not mess with this one.

When hiring for a server position, I'll have the applicant tell me what makes a particularly great dining experience for him or her, then to tell me what makes a poor experience. The answers will surprise you and shed light on his or her feelings toward service. When an interviewee tells me she loves it when the hostess is prompt and friendly with her greeting, that she is seated quickly, and that the service is great and her glass "never gets less than half full" or something to that effect, I know that this person is internally interested in good service and knows what it should look like. Most normal people will give as they like to receive, and, if everything else in our interview is good and she has the qualities listed below, the chances are very good that I'll be able to train her easily and she will be an excellent server. A similar line of questioning works for any position in the restaurant. Develop a script for yourself and use it for every interview. By law you are not allowed to write on an application, so print this script and take notes on it. Throughout your interview you will observe your candidate's demeanor—is he or she animated and smiling and looking you in the eye, or does he or she stare at the ground while answering your questions. There are a handful of traits experienced interviewers look for during the interview process.

So what are the traits we look for? Just some of the things we try to assess are the applicants' emotional stability, maturity, motivation, judgment, attitudes and ability to express themselves. Further we look for self-confidence, pleasant personal appearance and openness. The above mock interview demonstrated all of this. Another important area is the candidate's work history. Always remember that past behavior is a very reliable predictor of future behavior. Frequently skipping from job to job or conflict with previous managers will likely be repeated again and again in this person's career. Also, if a candidate previously made substantially more than you are able to offer, you will only be a temporary fix until something better comes along. Learn to spot all of these red flags along the way and professionally decline to employ that person.

There are five main characteristics that will indicate whether the candidate possesses the above traits. Those characteristics are:

1) Intelligence
2) Honesty
3) Motivation/drive/energy
4) Ability to communicate
5) Pleasant appearance

If you will listen and observe during the interview process, you will get a sense whether or not your candidate possess these qualities. Are his or her responses to your queries well thought out and communicated? This would indicate intelligence and communication skills. Is the prospect dressed in an acceptable manner? That would indicate he values his appearance and his image. Does your candidate appear energetic? Does she look you in the eye as she speaks with you? These things would suggest whether or not she has drive and energy and also good communication skills. Finally, is there consistency in everything the candidate says and does? This would indicate integrity or honesty.

There is one more area that is less understood, but no less important, that bears discussion here. Prior to offering the applicant a job, the manager must convey what the job entails in clear detail so that you match the applicant's expectation of the job with the reality of the job. Let me explain. One of the greatest problems our business faces is high turnover and a great portion of this is due to unmet or just wrong expectations. Many studies have been done on the subject and I will cite a case here that comes from an important reference book called *Applying Psychology In Business* by John Jones, Brian Steffy and Douglas Bray. This case is relevant to us and I think you will understand why.

This case dealt with an inventory taking company, which we'll call ABC. ABC was recruited by other companies to come and count inventories. ABC hired many people for the position of inventory-taker, and this position had extremely high turnover. After years of frustration, ABC hired a management consulting firm to study the problem of high turnover in this position and make recommendations to fix it. The firm began by conducting exit interviews and interviewing those still on the job. What the firm found was that in every case the job did not match the employee's expectation. During the "tell and sell" portion of the interview where ABC told the applicant about the company and the job they were being offered, the prospect wasn't told of the negative aspects of the job including poor/ dangerous work environments, resentment by employees of the companies they inventoried and longer than expected hours due to others calling in or quitting without notice. (Note: Some of these very issues are confronted in the restaurant business every day.)

After the consulting firm organized their information, five important areas emerged that needed to be covered in greater detail prior to ABC making a job offer to an applicant: (1) physical working conditions (2) social relations with managers, coworkers and customers (3) hours of work (4) duties and company policies (5) career opportunities. Next the firm devised a test to determine the effects of more accurate expectations. Job applicants for the job of inventory-taker were randomly assigned to one of two groups. The first group (alpha) ended up with 15 members. Prior to the job offer they were given written a **job preview** that clearly covered those five areas listed above. Those members of this group who would accept a job offer would also receive a verbal **job preview** during orientation. The second (beta) control group ended up with 13 members who were to be hired and oriented in the typical way that ABC always had used, with no job preview. All other training of members of both groups would be exactly the same. Here is where it gets interesting. The consulting firm was interested to see whether members of alpha group would be more likely to turn down job offers than those in beta group. As expected, four of the 15 members of alpha group turned down the job offer, but none of the beta group members did so. So now you have alpha group with 11 members who accepted the job and beta group with all 13 members who have accepted the job. Remember ABC's goal is to reduce turnover. After three months, seven of the 11 original members (64%) of alpha group were still working while only two of the 13 in beta group (15%) were still employed. The point of the story is that very clear and concise information covering key areas of importance to employees should be given up front in the form of a **job preview** to match employee's expectations with the reality of the job in order to reduce turnover.

So what does all that mumbo-jumbo mean? Let me break it down for you. It's called expectation management and this is how it works: Out front, in the interview process, let all prospective employees know that the work is really hard. I always try to scare them off with some graphic image of cleaning a toilet or heavy lifting. Then, as they settle into the job, they discover that it is not nearly as hard as you had said. That makes for a happy employee. Conversely, if you tell them the job's a piece of cake (and NO job is), they will be miserable at the first difficult patch. Always play up a job's difficulty up front. If you can learn how to interview and set expectations with humor and levity, you will set the feeling in your new employee that you are a fair and firm, but also a fun boss. This could be the beginning of something beautiful.

As stated above, hiring correctly is without a doubt the single most important thing we do. You can never educate yourself too much on this subject and it has received very limited treatment here. Any serious business owner or manager should take it upon him or herself to further his/her understanding of this very serious task. I created the following grid to assist you in your hiring process. It is by no means foolproof, but it will help you. In the end you have to make decisions that you are happy with, but you should do so armed with as much information as possible. You can also find helpful materials on our website at www.cookingwithgas.net.

Cooking With Gas Selection Matrix

Points	0	1	2	Score
Time on previous job	0 -months	9 months-2years	2years +	
Time at address	Less than 6 mos.	6 mos.- 1 year	Over 1 year	
Previous salary history	Over $8 an hr.	$7-8 per hr.	Min to $7 per hr.	
5 Qualities	None apparent	Some apparent	All apparent	
Interview	Negative attitudes detected	Neutral	Positive attitude detected	
			Total	

0 to 3 = no hire
4 to 6 = maybe
7 to 10 = good hire possible

You may need to adjust the previous salary history for your market. If the entry level salary is higher than minimum wage in your area, then adjust those figures in all three columns starting with the far right column under the heading 2. Say the minimum you pay is $8 per hour. You'll need to make that column read $8 per hour to $9.50 per hour, moving left $9.50 per hour to $11 per hour and so on. In time you internalize all these bits of information and they become second nature. There is no magic bullet, but these things will help. Your gut plays a part too. One last piece of advice, and then we will move on. When a person expresses that he or she just has to have a job because he/she is desperate, sadly, you cannot hire that person. That will always be a hire you will regret and you will rue the day you did it. Desperate people do desperate things. They are disorganized and bring great disruption to the workplace and then, just as quickly as they came, they are gone, leaving a trail of mess for you to clean up.

Once you have selected the correct employee, the next important (second in importance only to selection) step is:

<u>Training</u> —Good training begins with orientation. This crucial task is often completely overlooked or done in a

haphazard fashion, meaning that after all of the effort to select the right person we turn around and promptly drop the ball. Remember, good, happy employees are our single greatest asset. Without them we would be nowhere, so it is important that we treat them as such.

Entry into a new job can be frightening and stressful for most new employees. A professional orientation does much to allay those stressors. A good orientation introduces the new employee to the company, his or her co-workers, the first position he or she will be working and its relation to other areas of the business. This is also the time that you introduce the new employee to the company's rules and regulations laid out in your Team Member Handbook to minimize any risk of future disciplinary actions. Finally, this is the time that you explain how and when employees get paid, when the schedule is made and where it's posted, how and where to clock in and so forth. When properly done, orientation will relieve much of the anxiety of those first days on a new job and will help to reduce your turnover.

So how do we train? What method is best? Well, there are many methods out there, but the one that works best for "task" related duties is called "On The Job Training" (OJT) or the "three-step" method, and it works as follows:

1) The trainer explains the task while performing it.
2) Next the trainer performs the task while the trainee explains it.
3) Finally, the trainee both performs and explains the task.

Don't be surprised if it takes more than one time before the trainee masters the task, especially when he or she is new on the job.

Periodically it is necessary to review current employees' performance. Typically this is done quarterly, semi-annually or annually. This is called:

Performance Appraisal — The purpose of the appraisal is to measure actual performance against company standards (controlling function) in such areas as punctuality, flexibility in scheduling, cooperative spirit, teamwork, etc. The goal is to have all who are evaluated meet or exceed your standards in these areas. (To retain those that don't meet our standards is a great de-motivator to those who do.) In the course of business, employees' situations change; they move or get married and it is necessary to take care of the related administrative paperwork. This is called:

Human Resource Administration — As stated above, this involves filling out the proper forms to make any necessary changes to your employees' status. This may mean a new W-4 form or an address change. These matters are a very important responsibility of management and should not be overlooked.

An important point to make before we go on: You should have a policies and procedures manual which outlines all the do's and don'ts in your business. We furnish a really sexy one online at www.cookingwithgas.net. It has been developed over many years in this business. In your policies and procedures manual, you want every contingency covered as much as is humanly possible, and you want to enforce these with your staff. When employees don't perform to your standard, you should always document the infraction. Otherwise, you will have an employee folder filled with average to good performance appraisals and no evidence that this employee's performance was ever anything other than good to great. When the day comes that you need to terminate the employee, he or she will be able to point out that you have accepted this behavior in the past, as no evidence to the contrary exists in his or her employee folder. In fact, the folder is packed full of nothing but those positive performance appraisals. You will lose your case in unemployment court without supporting documentation, and your former employee will sit at home on the dole while you slave to pay your increased unemployment liabilities.

When an employee falls short, it is critical for that employee's well being that you take corrective action, and, believe it or not, you will have a better employee for it. For years my dentist has had a poster hanging on his wall that says, "You don't need to floss all your teeth, just the ones you want to keep." I guess it's kind of the same with people. In some cases, your corrective action fails. Certain people provide challenges that you as manager or owner cannot overcome. When that happens, it is your duty to terminate that employee. One bad employee will destroy morale in your restaurant and be a tremendous headache for you, so don't let the situation drag on. By the time a difficult employee's termination arrives it should be no surprise to him or anybody else; you have given him plenty of rope, and yet he has still managed to hang himself. As stated above, have a trail of preceding documented violations, do the termination privately, with another member of management as witness, and don't lose your cool. That employee may vent his spleen; he may spew vile anger or may go quietly with his tail between his legs. Your behavior should be the same regardless.

It is easy to see the four functions of management at work in the staffing system. As we proceed it becomes evident that in everything we do, especially when we do it successfully, we PLAN, ORGANIZE, INFLUENCE AND CONTROL. Once you have hired, oriented and trained a new employee the next thing that needs to be done is to incorporate him or her into the TEAM. But do you even have a team in your restaurant? Just because you have a group of people on your schedule does not necessarily mean you have a team, and if you don't have a team, you are performing inefficiently. The next section will deal with motivation, teams, team development and team maintenance.

Motivation

You can't lead by shoving. You can't scream and yell. You can't force people to do anything in this or any business. It is up to you to foster, within each employee, the desire to want to put forth effort. You must lead by example and get them to want to follow you. A good leader is firm but respects his employees. Each individual controls his or her own work effort and when you try force you will encounter the resistance of inertia.

Theories abound on what motivation is and how it is achieved. There are some common factors that most of the current literatures agree upon. First let's define workplace motivation. Motivation is "the willingness to put forth effort in pursuit of organization goals." Remember that the <u>individual alone controls his work effort</u>; we can only attempt to *influence* those efforts through our understanding of motivation. The link between productivity and motivation is well established and documented. Since our goal is positive productivity, it can easily be seen that we cannot achieve that goal by negative means. Fear will alter some people's behavior, but it is definitely not a good motivator. Fear only causes employees to try and not get into trouble, which is not the same as a willingness to put forth effort.

The key to motivation begins with selection. Carefully selecting the right players who exhibit the qualities mentioned above for your team is the first step to achieving a motivated workforce. Three components are crucial to individual performance.

1. The individual must have the capacity (ability) to perform.
2. He or she must possess some willingness to learn and perform.
3. Finally, we must provide the individual with the proper training, tools, and opportunity to perform.4.

We humans tend to perform better when rewards are attached to the outcomes of our efforts. Motivation theory says that there are two types of rewards that are important here:

a. <u>Extrinsic rewards</u> —These are outcomes that we positively value that are given by someone outside of ourselves in the workforce.
b. <u>Intrinsic rewards</u> —These are internally generated positive feelings derived as a result of good performance. In other words, feeling good about a job well done.c.

Intrinsic rewards are just what they suggest, a feeling of accomplishment. Extrinsic rewards operate much differently. Behavioral scientist B.F. Skinner outlined his theory of **Positive Reinforcement**[2] for behavioral modification in the workplace.

It is a very simple, but powerful theory that goes something like this: "The administration of positive consequences for desirable behavior tends to increase the likelihood of future desirable behavior in a similar setting." Translation, treat people well when they do a job you are happy with and they will likely duplicate that performance under similar circumstances. Positive rewards fall into two categories:

1. Contrived —These rewards have a cost attached to them and include such things as merit pay increases, allowing music in the workplace, parties for employees, etc. The costs for contrived rewards vary greatly, but all cause greater motivation.

2. Natural —This category includes such things as smiles at subordinates, greetings, the showing of respect to subordinates, compliments, recognition, etc. There are no direct costs attached to natural rewards and they are the greater motivator by far.

Another aspect of positive reinforcement is to focus (reinforce) on the behavior you want and always deal in positive terms. When a subordinate doesn't measure up, rather than phrasing in negatives such as, "you didn't need to do..." or "you shouldn't have..." always phrase in positives. What is meant here is that where performance is not what you expected, explain to your employee the behavior you expect rather than what was done wrong, thereby making the reinforcement positive rather than negative.

Remember, the individual alone controls his or her work effort. What we are attempting to do is to *influence* those efforts. The impact of powerful techniques such as positive reinforcement just makes sense if you think about it.

When the right people are hired and properly trained and motivated, we next turn our attention to team development.

All About Teams

What constitutes a team? When is a group a team, when are they not a team and how do we tell the difference? These are not easy questions to answer. Just like anything else, the knowledge of team development is a learned skill, but the rewards of having a cohesive, well functioning team make the learning of this skill well worth anyone's time. What follows is a brief description of what a team is, the stages of team development and how teams are maintained.

A team is defined as "a small group of people with complimentary skills, who work together to achieve a common purpose for which they hold themselves collectively accountable." In many ways a team resembles a person. It has an existence, needs feedback in the form of positive reinforcement for good work and corrective guidance when off-course. What the team possesses that makes it unique is **synergy.** Synergy is defined as "the creation of a whole that is greater than the sum of its parts." Where synergy occurs, the group accomplishes more than the total of its members' individual capabilities. Here are just a few positive attributes of teams:

- Teams are good for the individuals that comprise them.
- Teams generate creative solutions to problems better than individuals.
- Teams exert control over their members.
- Synergy, synergy, synergy.

For our purposes teams have four distinct stages. They are:

1. **Forming** —This is the stage where a group first comes together. It is characterized by a lack of unifying purpose and goals, lack of cooperation, a general sense that everyone is pulling his or her own way. A group, regardless of how long it has been together, can stay in the forming stage. You probably won't have to look too far to see groups at this stage.

2. **Storming** —The next stage in a team's life is called storming. This is where in-fighting and battling takes place to establish a pecking order. It is here that members' **roles** (expected behaviors within the group) begin to form.

3. **Norming** —This is where "norms" for the group begin

to evolve. A norm is a standard of behavior expected of each team member by his fellow team members. Teams become self-policing through their norms and according to the level of cohesiveness of the team; deviations from the norms are not tolerated.

4. **Performing** —This takes place when the team is a cohesive, functioning group with common purpose and goals. This is where real synergy takes place. Here, everyone's load is made lighter by the cooperation of the greater group. This is the goal of every great manager or coach.

In environments like the restaurant business with lots of entry and exit of members, teams tend to be in the more immature stages of development. That is one reason that we must work diligently at understanding and building teams. So where do we start? How do we proceed? The logical place to start is at the beginning.

Team Building

Team building is a sequence of planned activities designed to foster the functioning of a team, improve teamwork and increase productivity. First, the objectives for the work group must be defined. In our case that would be effective operations of the restaurant. Next, a person in a leadership role must convey the objectives to the group and encourage its members to work together to accomplish these objectives. Work early and often with teams to establish a high standard of **norms** for the members to internalize. We as leaders must do all that we can to foster an environment of creativity and participation. Plan team meetings and encourage the group to answer the question, "how well are we doing terms of task accomplishment?" Have your team critique their performance and then have them develop action plans to facilitate improvement. As your team coalesces, encourage them to monitor progress and be self-policing.

Certain activities are required to maintain teams. These are called "team maintenance activities." These types of activities support the "emotional" life of the group. These activities may include:

- *Encouraging* —praising, accepting or agreeing with other members' ideas, which demonstrates togetherness and warmth.
- *Harmonizing* —mediating squabbles within the group; facilitating reconciliation and compromise. Also may include keeping some members from dominating the group.
- *Setting standards*— —expressing standards for the group to use in evaluating its group process.
- *Guiding* —providing clear guidance when the team strays from its objectives.
- *Culling* —It is critical that you remove non-performers who fail to meet set standards from the team. One bad apple...Culling reminds those who stay on that you are serious about company standards. Your team will rally.

All teams must be comprised of members who feel a sense of responsibility to actively work together to accomplish the goals that they have set forth. From the beginning and through all stages teams face many challenges including entry/exit of members, disgruntled members, etc. It can easily be seen that with a hands-on approach by someone who understands these dynamics, strong, vibrant teams can be developed that bring creative solutions and greater productivity to your business and greater satisfaction to all.

Another important activity for the maintenance of your team is a scheduled team meeting. Use these meetings to hold training or re-training sessions to brush up on company policies and procedures, particularly those polices and procedures that may have been violated lately. Team meetings are also the best time to notify staff of menu or price changes, and most importantly, team meetings are an awesome place to recognize and reward great performance on the part of one or more team members.

There it is: the functions of management. Okay, maybe it

ain't quite the same as a four-year degree in Business College, but it's a start. You have learned the importance of planning, how to use internal controls to manage food and labor costs, and what it means to hire, train, motivate and form teams to do the work.

Now that you've got them hired and trained you are ready to open your doors. However, there are just a couple more things we need to talk about.

Quickfax

- *Have standards for your business set forth in your Team Member Handbook and other written materials.*
- *Select the correct employee for the job using your skills as a great interviewer.*
- *Give every new hire a job preview with realistic job descriptions and state your expectations of each employee.*
- *Orient and train all employees the same way.*
- *Build teams. Perform team maintenance activities to keep team morale high.*
- *Cull from the team those that perform below written standards.*
- *NYCWG!*

Chapter 8

The Bully Twins (food and labor)

I f you don't take these two seriously, they will mug you, then shove you under the bus and leave you for dead. If you live, you'll be broke, and, I promise, you'll wish you were dead. The Bully Twins I refer to are, of course, your two biggest controllable costs: food and labor. If you fail to control these two, they will quickly control you (think Delila). We have talked some about these two in previous chapters, but they are so important, they deserve further treatment. They are presented here in the order they will appear on your income statement.

Food

As described in the chapter on financial statements, food appears on your income statement as a line item called "cost of goods sold." It's the cost of items used during that period. If you are a good operator, you will be tracking your food usage on a weekly basis using a food inventory worksheet, working with some kind of variance sheet, and you will be fanatical about it. You have to be. Your inventory worksheet takes beginning inventory for the week, adds all received products[3], and then subtracts out ending inventory for the week. The difference is food used for the week. Example:

Chicken Wings:

Beginning Inventory	+	Received	=	Total Available	-	Ending Inventory	=	Used
25		50		75		22		53

The food used is then multiplied by the cost per unit, for example, 53 x $5.75 = $304.75 to arrive at the "extended cost." All extended costs for every item of inventory you carry are then added up to arrive at your total food cost in dollars. This dollar figure is then divided by sales for the same period to arrive at that magic percentage we in the business call "food cost." When I call my friend who owns a restaurant across town and ask her what her food cost is, she will always answer with a percentage; for example, 31%. To which I would reply that that was great and I might ask her how she accomplished this. There is a range on what constitutes normal food cost and it lies between 27% and 37%. A decent average food cost percent is 33%. That means that of every dollar that crosses your counter in sales, 33 cents is spent on food. How relevant is this? Let me tell you, it is critical to your success. Poor understanding of food and labor costs is the main reason most restaurants go out of business. Study these numbers and get to know them inside and out. When you track your food cost, you are in touch with the flow of your food items. You can spot what's moving and what's not, and you will catch any anomaly. An unexplained high usage in an item coupled with a low sales yield (you learned about yields in the *controls* section of the management chapter) could well point to a theft problem. Many people have failed in this business because they failed to use these tools. While a food cost that is too high indicates waste through over-portioning, thoughtlessness, and perhaps even theft, a food cost that is too low may indicate chronic under-portioning. If that is the case, you have been cheating your customers, but, trust me, your customer won't let that go on for too long.

Food usage has three components:

1. Sold: The product you sell is also often called "theoretical usage" in POS systems. This component is the largest portion of the food used during a period.

It represents all foods sold and this information is provided for you by your POS system.

2.   Waste: Usually the second largest component of food usage. Always expect some waste, but one of the greatest areas of loss is over-portioning by careless employees. Always track the waste of key items. Remember in the variance report that you allow for waste and calculate the difference between optimal usage and actual usage. The difference is what is unaccounted for (missing).

3.   Missing: Is that portion of usage that we cannot account for. We sold one unit and wasted .05 of a unit, but at the end of the week, upon completion of our inventory we discover we used 2.05 units; we have exactly one unit that is unaccounted for. Where did it go? That's a good question. It could be that you miscounted your inventory, entered one more into inventory received than was actually received, or, maybe you have a pilferage problem.

Whatever the case, if you don't understand any of this when you get into this business, you start with the greatest of handicaps. You will never have any idea of what is really going on in your business and you will lose you shirt. For your convenience we provide helpful spreadsheets to aid you in tracking your sales, labor, food cost and variances on line at www.cookingwithgas. net. Nothing fancy or flashy, just straightforward, easy to use spreadsheets to help you get the job done.

How to set menu pricing: This is a frequently asked question and I will attempt to provide some guidance here. First check your competition and see where they fall for similar product. Remember, we like to keep food cost percentage somewhere around 33% (target a range between 27% and 37% for food items) and the formula is cost of food used divided by net sales. Let me say that again. **Food cost = cost of goods used ÷ net sales.**

So if the formula for food cost is cost ÷ sales = percentage, let's work that formula backwards to help price a single item.

Say you are opening Bud's Burgers and you want to price your burger. In order to do so, you would take the cost of everything that makes up the burger—the patty, the bun, 1 oz. mayo, 1 oz. ketchup, ½ oz mustard[4], lettuce, tomato, pickle and cheese—and add those up. Total cost to you to assemble one hamburger with all the toppings = $1.00. Remember, you want that $1.00 to end up as 33% of sales so if you use a factor of 300% you get: $1.00 x 3 = $3.00. So you should sell your burger at about $3.00, and, being the crafty business person that you are, you would probably price your burger at $2.99 (of course making sure that this is in keeping with similar products sold at your competitor's nearby).

While we are at it, you wanted to price a regular portion of French fries so let's do it too. Say you have decided to serve a three-ounce (3 oz.) portion as your regular order. The fries come frozen, six bags to a case, 36 pounds per case, with a case costing $44.16. How much are you going to charge for your regular (3-oz.) size? Let's do the math: one bag of fries weighs six pounds or 96 ounces, which equates to 32 three-ounce portions, and the bag costs $7.36. So, the cost to you for one portion of fries is $7.36 ÷ 32 = 23 cents per three-ounce serving, plus the cost of the bag which the fry is portioned into (.002 cents). Using the same rule as in the burger example: cost x 300% = .232 x 3 = a price point of 69 cents for your regular portion of French fries and again you would check to see that this in keeping with the local competition. This method works best for average items. High ticket items such as expensive steak or lobster may have a slightly lower margin and higher food cost. For example, if I pay $15 for a premium grade filet mignon and use the same formula $15 x 3 = $45 it is unlikely anybody will pay $45 for that steak no matter how good it is. I will have to accept a smaller profit margin on that menu item. The flip side of that coin is certain low cost items, such as carbonated beverages, some frozen dessert items, etc. For example, certain frozen pies may cost 17 cents and using the formula we see that .17 x 3 = 51 cents. That same pie sells for 79 cents all over town. What do you think I'm gonna sell it for? That's right, 79 cents. That gives me a good margin which offsets the high margin on other items and hopefully, if I'm doing things right, I'll come out with a decent food cost at the end of the day!

The 33% average food cost assumes normal ranges on other costs, such as rent and other overhead, etc., and it does not include alcohol. Pricing on alcohol is fairly standard and guidelines are suggested by vendors. There are other methods for menu item pricing and, by all means, you should ferret them out, but at least you now have an idea of what you are looking at. Also, if you are a franchisee, your franchisor will have recommended pricing and will provide you with information on standard food cost for the company. Although the franchisor may not provide appropriate administrative paperwork for you to track sales, food, labor, etc., that's all right because you know you can log on to www.cookingwithgas.net and find whatever you need.

The next bully that will leave you broke on the side of the road if you don't control him is:

Labor

Typically called payroll, labor is the second largest controllable cost. It is important that you come to understand and control it as well. Just as above, if you are a good operator, you are going to track, monitor and analyze payroll all of the time and be fanatical about it so that everyone who works for you, your managers and employees, take it seriously. Remember, they watch what you watch; if you don't watch anything, well guess what! As in the food cost example above, payroll is usually expressed as a percent. So what exactly is payroll? Payroll is the total dollars paid out to all employees during a period of time divided by the net sales for that same period. So yesterday I paid employees $660 and my sales for the day were $3000. My payroll when stated as a percentage is 22%, which for most restaurants would be considered good, for some it may even be considered great. Added onto your raw payroll dollars are payroll taxes, which we will touch on in a later chapter.

All payroll begins with a schedule and it is one of the most important tools in your restaurant. If you don't understand the importance of controlling payroll, you will craft a poor schedule. Delila scheduled anybody and everybody all of the time with no awareness of the costs. By the time you begin to understand, it's too late, and understanding this subject takes some time.

The normal range of payroll in the restaurant business is between 22% and 33% depending on several factors, most importantly, of course, your level of sales. The slower you are, the harder it is to hold that percentage down. Even when you do everything else right, you are still going to need employees to open and close the restaurant and those are nonproductive times from a sales standpoint. But, for the sake of this conversation, let's call 25% "normal." You would like to land on 25% week after week, but how to do it? Remember, the formula is **payroll dollars ÷ net sales = payroll percent.** Let's look at in terms of a single person. Your average employee makes $7 per hour.[5] That $7 payroll for one person needs to represent 25% of some number, say $7 ÷ x = 25% When you do the math the number you come up with is $28 ($7 ÷ .25 = $28); therefore, for every labor hour worked you need to generate $28 in sales. That $28 is called **productivity.** As long as your average hourly salary remains $7 and you generate $28 per hour your payroll will be 25% every day during productive time. In other words, while you are open. However, there are a few hours of nonproductive time before you open and after you close. These hours have no sales associated with them, so we must adjust our productivity upward just a little to accommodate these nonproductive hours. A 15% adjustment upward on the productivity should cover the down times, but you can always adjust this either way. So if your average hourly salary tells you that you need $28 in productivity, then a simple adjustment: $28 x 1.15 = $33 (rounded up) gives you a productivity that covers your nonproductive as well as your productive times. *NYCWG!*

Okay, so you tell me your payroll is currently 36%. I'll tell you your schedule is too fat. It has too many hours on it and you are inefficient. Right now your productivity is $19.44 per hour worked (assuming a $7 hourly wage). You need to improve efficiency by tweaking your schedule and ratcheting back the hours while keeping sales the same. Keep in mind that if you have been operating like this for some time, your employees will absolutely think you are trying to kill them, so you may want to take the revision slow. Now that you know that at the current average hourly wage a $33 productivity yields approximately a 25% payroll, you figured out that if you take your projected sales for the coming week and divide them by productivity, you will have the number of hours you need to schedule for the coming week. It is so simple: $30,000 ÷ $33 = 909 hours you can schedule and you can bank it that by the end of the week, if you do near $30,000 and you use around 909 hours, payroll will right on the money. You can see that productivity is a yield on human labor. Do you get it? *NYCWG!* So let's summarize:

Average hourly salary = total payroll dollars ÷ total hours worked.

Productivity = sales generated per man hour worked.

Projected sales = an average of past sales, usually four weeks.

Projected sales ÷ productivity = allotted hours for the week.

Projected sales divided by productivity = allotted hours

$10,000 ÷ $33	= 303 hours
$11,000 ÷ $33	= 334 hours
$12,000 ÷ $33	= 364 hours

Do you want to tighten your belt a little further? Let's say you want to achieve a 22% payroll (a worthy aspiration), same formula as before: $7 ÷ x = 22%. $7 ÷ .22 = $32. Now take $32 x 1.15 = $37 and $37 is your new productivity.

$10,000 ÷ $37	= 270 hours
$11,000 ÷ $37	= 298 hours
$12,000 ÷ $37	= 325 hours

You notice fewer hours in the second example for each set of sales because you are now trying to lower your overall payroll rate. That is essentially what a matrix is; a list of projected sales and the allotted hours for those sales. Knowledge is power and this is powerful knowledge. These are more tools for you to put into your tool kit. As with everything there is a part science and a part art. This is the science part, but there is also nuance and finesse in this business too. You may add a little here or take away a little there. Always train yourself and managers to trim the staff during the slow periods of the day such as the dead period between 2:00pm and 5:00pm. If you own a low volume restaurant, you will always battle high payroll, even when you work it yourself. Don't be discouraged; just continue to work on it. Schedule carefully.

A few more points regarding payroll. You have to be ever-vigilant and strict because many employees will attempt to take advantage of you by abusing your time clock and some of these tricks are hard to fight. Here are just a few ways this is done:

- Employee walks in for his shift not in uniform and goes right for the time clock, clocks in then disappears into the restroom for a 20-minute changing and primping session.
- Extreme amounts of time taken in restroom.
- Breaks taken without clocking out.
- Employee leaves her shift but has a friend clock her out later.
- Employee finishes shift, goofs off, goes and changes back out of his uniform, etc., then clocks   out.
- If you don't pay attention, they will be in their cars listening to the radio or even sleeping.
- Just as a payroll too high is bad for you, a payroll too low is bad for your guests. If your normal payroll averages 24%, but as you look over yesterday's numbers you realize payroll for the day was 17.50%, you may rest assured of a couple of things:
- You operated yesterday "shorthanded," which means that probably a couple of people did not show for work.
- As a result, your guests did not get the service to which they are accustomed and this is almost never a good thing (the only time it would be good is if the service to which they are accustomed is poor, and, by

chance, they actually received good service on this day. Stranger things have happened!)

Consequently a payroll too low is as bad for long-term prospects as a payroll that's too high.

Don't let these twins bully you! You be the bully. You have no choice, for your success depends upon it! I know that you are soaking this up like a sponge! I know you're getting it. *NYCWG!*

Now, all that being said, let's flip the coin over and look at the other side(then put the coin back in your pocket and keep it there). Earlier we said that every dollar saved in controllable costs, while keeping sales the same, flows through to the bottom line. What if we continued to watch those controllable costs and, at the same time, created incremental growth? Mind you, your controllable costs are what is known as variable costs, so naturally, if you are selling more food you will be spending more dollars on food. Remember, though, it's the percentage you are concerned with. By getting those percentages down, you have increased your profit margin. So, as sales grow, variable costs like food and labor dollars naturally do the same, but fixed costs like rent and certain overhead stay the same, so you can see that a large portion of your incremental growth will "flow through" to the bottom line.

What are some of the ways to improve sales, you might ask? Great question, I answer. Broadly speaking there are two ways: one that incurs additional expense and, hopefully, will bring in new customers. It's called advertising. The other does not add additional expense and deals with the customers you already have.

- Let's start with the one that does not incur additional expense because that is where you should start. In the "quick service" (the new euphemism for fast food) industry, where I have spent most of my restaurant life, people are in a hurry. Americans are busier than ever and we work more hours per week than any other industrialized nation. People have less and less time to go to the grocery store, shop, return home, unload, put away, prepare a meal and clean up. Those things eat up a lot of time and money. It is actually cheaper for a family to grab a bucket of chicken or a bag of burgers. We restaurateurs provide a very important product and service to busy Americans. So time is an important commodity. Follow this story, because it's one I use in training service personal to make a point and to relieve some of the natural squeamishness some people have about selling.

Aaron is on his lunch break. After making a quick stop at the bank and post office, half his break is gone. His goal was to come to my fast food restaurant and order his entree, a medium drink and the chocolate pudding coconut cream pie that only I sell and which he loves, but now he's frazzled and rushed because of time wasted at the bank. He stands in my restaurant line for another couple of minutes, irritated, and then finally gets to the counter and orders his entree, and my server abruptly says, in a non-courteous fashion and through her bubblegum, *"Is that it?"* Well right there she has shut him down; she just closed the spigot. He's harried, running late, and her abruptness caused him to forget to order his drink and pie, so he replies *"yes"*, she tells him the total, collects money, and I just lost a large portion of that transaction. This incident is repeated time and time again all over the country, and it is very costly.

Let me digress for one second. There are a couple of expressions that are not to be spoken in any restaurant that I am associated with, and, contrary to everything I have said about being a firm and fair boss (which I am, usually), these expressions really set me off. One is the expression above: "Is that it?" or "Is that all?" or any variation thereof. I become Attila the Hun whenever I hear them. I developed the story of Aaron to help my employees understand that we are not forcing our guests to buy something extra, rather we are reminding them of what they intended to buy in the first place. We help them to "round out" the meal: main course, drink and dessert. Our guests need our help because of the limited time they have. Set in those terms, most reasonable employees really understand.

Always teach your service personnel, even in the quick service environment, to find a way to touch on main course, drink and dessert with every customer. It can be done. And never, ever, under any circumstances, allow them to end with—*"is that all?"* A courteous close, after you have done the above, is to ask if that will complete the order. This is called suggestive sales or add-on sales. It costs you nothing additionally, but will create great incremental growth to your bottom line. Before you do anything else, master this. Give yourself a raise today!

- Another very important way to give yourself a pop to the bottom line is to pick a menu item with a low food cost, such as a medium drink or cherry pie, and have a sales contest with this item. First of all you have to determine a minimum number to be sold; any number below that is disqualified from the contest. Typically you might add somewhere between 25% and 50% on top of average sales per server. Build the contest up for a week or two in advance and run the contest for at least a month. Track the contest on a jazzy tracking chart that you design, so that all your team members can follow it and razz one another. The results? WOW, you will not believe the results: greater team spirit and a good hit to your bottom line.

Let's use cherry pie for the example. The pie costs me 14 cents and I sell it for 79 cents (penny profit: 79 cents —14 cents = 65 cents; food cost of 17.72%). An added bonus: there is very little in the way of payroll associated with preparation. I have 12 servers and each sells on average 150 pies per month; that's a total of 1,800 pies per month or about five pies per server per day. Now I know this is weak, so I am going to set the minimum at 50% above the average pie sales per server: 150 x 1.5 = 225 pies. The person who sells the most pies over 225 wins $150! Whoa, a hundred and fifty dollars you scream; that sounds like a lot of money. Well, consider two things:

1. You want to get people excited and to do that you need to sweeten the pot and share the wealth. One caveat: You will need to monitor that enthusiasm.

If you aren't careful, some employees will take it a little too far and really twist customers' arms to buy more pies, but for the most part it's a lot of fun. Your employees will co-opt their regular customer into the game, that customer will want to buy as many pies as possible from Jenny, her favorite server, to help her win.

2.   Do the math: at a minimum, if each server only sells 225 pies, that's 2,700 pies. Let's do some figuring.

Normal sales (150) pies	225 pies	300 pies
1800*.65 = $ 1,170	2700*.65 = $ 1,755	3600 * .65 = $ 2,340
	$ (1,170)	$ (1,170)
	$ 585	$ 1,170
	Prize $ $ (150)	Prize $ $ (150)
	$ 435	$ 1,020

As long as you keep interest up and every server sells the minimum—and they will—the least that flows through is $435. I don't know about you, but $435 sounds good to me. If you double pie sales, $1,020 will trickle down to the bottom line. Not bad and everyone had such a great time that they will be looking for the next contest!

Training your staff for suggestive sales and initiating contests are just two ideas to help boost profits. There are many others. For example, consider the following:

•   Similar to the above examples is a "check average contest." The check average is the dollar sales per customer over the course of a shift for each server. The check average is calculated by dividing that server's total net sales by her customer count. This is a very revealing number because it shows you who's hot and who's not. You will know right away that Marcy is really on top of her game and doing things the way you want her to and that it looks like Trish is asleep at the wheel. As in the pie example, you determine the minimum check average and prize and then let the fun begin. Okay, now you are cooking with gas, all pistons are firing. You are controlling costs and building sales with the customers you currently have. Now let's branch out.

- The other method of boosting profits mentioned above was advertising and this one entails some expense, but it is a necessary evil. You have to let your prospective customer know that you exist, and advertising is the main way to bring new customers in the door and increase sales. There are many mediums for advertising and here I will enumerate a few.

- TV —Network can be very expensive, but in many markets, it is the driving force. Cable is a little more reasonable, but you may not reach as many potential customers. Before you do this, talk with other restaurateurs you may know to find out which way has worked best for them. If you are a franchise owner, the franchisor will more than likely do the advertising in your market for you. If not, he or she will assist you in the decision making process. That's what you pay that advertising royalty for.

- Radio —Radio is an important medium in urban areas where there is high "drive-time." For example, cities where commuters spend a half hour or more commuting to work. If your area doesn't have such traffic, then radio may not be the most effective medium for you. Also radio can be as expensive as TV. Radio is now big conglomerate with two or three companies owning all stations in a market. Under one roof, they may have country, hip-hop, talk radio, top hits, oldies, etc. If you opt for radio, make sure all of your air time is directed to the genre that best fits your demographic. You wouldn't advertise your neighborhood mom & pop malt shop on the urban hip-hop station. The better fit for you would be the oldies station.

- Newspaper —There are two ways to go in the newspaper. One is to take out an ad in the paper; the second is called a free-standing-insert (FSI in the lingo), which is a coupon that you have labored to create and then had printed at great expense. It is then inserted in the paper on Sunday. The problem here is that when most people open the paper all the coupons fall to the floor. They pick them up in a wad and throw them in the trash, never seeing that precious piece that you labored over and paid an arm and a leg for; printing costs can sometimes be exorbitant.

- Direct mail coupons —This is a decent way to go because you can target specific zip codes to market directly to your demographic. Again, the printing can be expensive, so make sure you shop it around.

After you are up and running and doing things right, the most important form of advertising of all will begin to pick up momentum and you have probably guessed that I'm talking about: word-of mouth. For good or for bad, word-of-mouth will have the most impact on your business over the long run.

So, let's summarize this chapter. Food and labor costs need to be kept in line. When costs are too high, it's an indication of poor management, and when costs are too low, your customer is being cheated either by under-portioning or understaffing. When you tame those Bully Twins and bring those costs into line, you send money straight to the bottom line. At the same time, work on enhancing every sale that you currently have through building check averages, side items sales, in-house contests because you'll be sending even more money to the bottom line—all with no additional costs. Research the different forms of advertising and their costs and try to develop a mix and a strategy that you are comfortable with. You getting it? *NYCWG!*

While you are managing costs and building sales, you will also have to ensure that each guest receives great product and great service all in a sparkling clean environment. That's easy for me to say.

Chapter 9

Quality, Service & Cleanliness

What do you mean you've never heard of The Holy Trinity in the restaurant business? When you set your mission statement, it likely included a reference to one or more of the "big three." The restaurant business has an infinite array of concepts from a single drive-thru serving to-go food only, to fine dining establishments where nicely dressed patrons are seated by a tuxedoed maitre d' in a swanky, plush environment. No matter what the concept, all restaurants have three fundamental aspects in common. These are known as the Big Three: Quality Product, Quality Service and Quality Cleanliness called simply Q, S & C in the business. Regardless of what type of restaurant you own, if you don't execute well in these areas, then all your efforts are wasted.

Product, service and cleanliness form an integrated whole. The Big Three are the pistons working together that drive this engine, and should any piston not be fully operational, the engine grinds to a halt. It's not enough that your food looks good and tastes good. Would you eat at a restaurant that provided good food, but had terrible service and was dirty? No. How about a restaurant whose service was decent, but the food was no good and the place was a mess? No again. So you can see how important it is to have systems in place to manage each of these areas individually so that each guest receives the experience he or she expects and perceives it as a value for the money spent. Let's break out each area individually, examine each, and then consider effective ways that we might measure our successes in these areas and take corrective action where necessary to improve the overall guest experience.

Quality Product:

Not only should your food look appealing and taste good, but it must also be safe. Keeping your food safe should be top priority and is a 24/7 proposition. We can only know with certainty what happens with food starting at the moment we receive it. Prior to that is anybody's guess. From the moment food leaves the processing plant until the time we serve it to the guest, it may be in the **Temperature Danger Zone** a combined total of four hours. Since you have no way of knowing what temperature that product has been held from the time of production until the time you receive it, you must never allow it to be held in the Temperature Danger Zone. The **Temperature Danger Zone** is 41 to 140 degrees and it is dangerous because in that temperature range bacteria in food will flourish. There is a path that food follows as it flows through your restaurant. Along that path are vulnerabilities to food safety and it is up to you to manage food through all phases. The following is the flow of food and some of the ways to keep food safe.

- **Receipt** —Food is received in three different forms: 1. Frozen. 2. Refrigerated and 3. Dry and then taken immediately into storage. Upon receipt, all food should be marked with the day, date and initials of the person receiving it. Always use FIFO (First-In-First-Out) rotation.
- **Storage**
- **Frozen** food is typically received at 0 degrees + / —5 degrees. Ideally it should come off the truck and go directly into your freezer. Under no circumstances should it ever be allowed to sit outside the freezer longer than 10 minutes. When receiving frozen food, look for evidence of defrosting or defrosting and refreezing; you can tell by the presence of ice crystals on the surface of food. If you determine either to be

the case, refuse the shipment as these will yield sub-standard finished product.

- **Refrigerated** food is received at 36 degrees + / − 2 degrees and ideally should go directly into refrigeration. It should also not be allowed to be out of refrigeration longer than 10 minutes.
- **Dry** food is received and placed into storage at 60 degrees + / − 10 degrees.
- **Preparation** — Usually at the beginning of each shift a "par prep" list is compiled of quantities of menu items that will need to be prepped for the coming shift. During preparation, food service workers must be careful to obey the rules of sanitation: all utensils and surfaces are sanitized before and after food preparation, hands are washed frequently and dried with single-use paper towels, never on an apron or with a linen towel. Gloves must always be worn for direct contact with food. Prepped food is either placed back in refrigeration or cooked immediately.
- **Cooking** — Always make sure utensils are clean, the griddle or grill is clean and up to temperature, and that the oil or shortening used for frying is filtered and up to the proper temperature. The following are important internal temperatures that meats should attain.
  - Rare beef should attain an internal temperature of 130 degrees.
  - Fish products are typically cooked to 140 degrees; however tuna may be served medium rare at 125 to 130 degrees.
  - Pork and any food containing pork should attain an internal temperature of 155 degrees and be fully cooked with clear running juices.
  - Ground meat should attain an internal temperature of 155 degrees. Don't even permit the option of medium rare or rare with ground meat.

- Poultry, venison, stuffed meats or stuffing containing meat must attain a temperature of 165 degrees and be fully cooked with clear running juices.
- Food should be cooked to prescribed temperatures; all cooked foods must be served at 140 degrees or above.
- **Holding** — Some food product will be cooked and then held on the line. It must stay at or above 140 degrees and should have a prescribed holding time. When food exceeds its holding   time, discard it.
- **Serve** —The point at which cooked food is brought to the customer. Hot foods are always a minimum of 140 and cold foods are always 41 degrees or below. Hot foods hot and cold foods cold. Yeah!
- **Save/cooling** — Some cooked foods such as soups and stews are cooled, refrigerated and used again. When this is the case, never take hot product directly to the walk-in cooler. There are several reasons for this. Number one is that the product will sour or spoil more quickly, and hot product can raise the temperature of your cooler to unsafe levels. The best method for cooling is to submerge the product in an ice bath to bring the temperature down rapidly and then refrigerate. Rapid cooling decreases the time the product spends in the Temperature Danger Zone.
- **Reheat** — Foods that are reheated to be served should be reheated to a minimum of 165 degrees for a minimum of 15 seconds.

When placing food in any of the above mentioned forms of storage, keep a few things in mind:

- Always store "ready-to-eat" foods above and away from raw foods.
- Always store all chemicals (cleaning supplies, bleach, pesticides, etc.) below and away from food products. It is best to give cleaning supplies their own shelf.

- All food, regardless of the form of storage, must be kept six inches off the floor and four inches from the wall.

In most states in the nation today, you, as a food service operator and whether manager or owner will be required to be certified in some form of food safety program. The most common is the Serve-Safe program presented by the National Restaurant Association. It is an 8-hour course with some fairly formidable information presented. Log on to: www. nraef.org/index.asp for further information regarding your state's requirements. Another great resource for food safety is the United States Food and Drug Administration's web site at www.fda.gov/default.htm. It is here that you will find the HACCP (Hazard Analysis and Critical Control Point) program. Eventually you will institute some form of that program in your kitchen.

Above was the briefest of introductions to food safety, and no doubt your head is already spinning. You might wonder "*how much of this do I really need to worry about?*" My friend, the answer is simple: one confirmed case of food-borne illness could put you out of business between the bad press and possible litigation. In the town where I live, our local newspaper prints all health department violators in a special segment of the paper. That's just bad for business, so you can see that it is vitally important to install systems for food safety from the very beginning and be absolutely uncompromising with your staff. No half-measures can be accepted. Health inspectors are a picky lot, but they have to be. They protect the public at large, and lives are literally at stake. When they come into your restaurant, walk with them, talk with them, take notes and don't argue; assure her or him that you will remedy any situation pointed out immediately, and, of course, you will, because he or she will pay you a follow-up visit within one month. Keep your food appealing and safe to keep you customer satisfied! Keep it safe to stay in business!

Quality Service:

The next piece of the puzzle that brings the picture of guest satisfaction a little more into focus is quality service. We have all been to that expensive restaurant where we plunked down big bucks only to be treated poorly. You know the routine: your drink is nearly empty and it's been so long since you last saw your server that your ice has even melted. You start by looking around. You lean way out of your booth...and then you really crane your neck to the point of nearly snapping. Just then a server whizzes past, and you wave and flail about. You may even utter some kind of peep or may even get out an *"excuse me, miss..."* but it's no use; the server acts as if she never saw you...and your meal hasn't even arrived yet. Then, of course, you get out of your booth, by this point agitated, go up to the front and ask if somebody could please refill your drinks. Well, needless to say, by the time that meal arrives, it has lost some of its appeal. Of course, the service continues in the same vein for the rest of the evening because now you are the big jerk-meanie. Even if the food is great, you are tired, your feet hurt, the kids are fussy and you won't be coming back to this restaurant anytime soon. Sound familiar? Of course it does, we have all been there. Don't let this be your restaurant.

Just as you have set up systems for food handling to keep it safe, you must set systems to ensure that each and every guest gets the service he or she deserves. If you are a franchise operation, those systems are spelled out for you, and they are measurable, but it is still your job to make sure they happen the way they are supposed to. However, if you are doing your own thing, you will set the systems. Whichever is the case, just as you are uncompromising about food safety, you must be uncompromising about service, and recall that it begins by hiring people who recognize what good service looks like (see chapter 7). You will need a standard greeting, a standard approach to each guest, a standard for order taking, a standard time it should take for the average meal to be served, and a standard thanking and invitation to each guest to return, and your staff must do each of these the same every time. By having a standard, you have something you can quantify and measure; more on that in a minute.

Here's how great service starts: create a **culture**[6] of genuine hospitality and talk about it often. Hospitality training doesn't end the day you train your employee, it starts there. It's an ongoing, ever-improving process. You need to feed, foster and train sensitivity to your guests' needs, and, of course, it starts with you. Have monthly team meetings and talk about it, have pre-rush meetings and talk about it. Teach your employees to read body language signs. In the example above, a member of the staff should have noticed the moment that guest turned her head to look for a server and promptly responded. Teach your employees that every guest that walks through the door is "their" guest; not just the guy sitting at a table in their station; every dish that comes out of the kitchen is "their" dish; not just the food going to the guest that they are waiting on. Teach them the following essentials that should be a part of every guest's experience:

- **Greeting:** A warm, sincere and friendly welcome with a big smile should greet each party; even better if your business name is included in the greeting, such as: *"Hi, welcome to Merrimack's..."* The same applies on the telephone and the drive-thru speaker. Teach your order taker to smile as she answers the phone or greets each guest on the drive-thru microphone. Yes, she will look at you like you're crazy the first time you tell her this, but she'll get it soon enough. If you are a full-service restaurant, your hostess will seat the guests or take their names and inform them of the wait time.

- **Introduction:** In full service your server should always say, *"Hi, my name is..."* or *"Hi, my name is...and I will be your server today"* and then proceed to ask if there are questions, and take the order if the guest is ready.

- **Maintenance:** Without being overbearing your servers should service your guests as the meal proceeds; be available, but invisible. When guests complete the meal, remove the plates, but not the glasses, unless told to and, again, try not to intrude.

- **Farewell:** As each guest leaves, hopefully smiling and making a joke about loosening his belt a notch or two, you and your staff always thank him and invite him to return.

In addition to a plan for service, you as owner or manager must have a recovery strategy when things go wrong, and, no matter how good you are, things will go wrong. Too often, the extent of recovery for many is that the manager, when informed of a complaint, will come out from the back of the restaurant, address the guest with a flat, uncaring: *"can I help you, ma'am?"* (think Sergeant Joe Friday of Dragnet), the guest explains her grievance, and, again, in the same monotone voice, the manager offers a refund. Flat. No love. No caring. That is not hospitality; it is the opposite of it. That manager just wants to be rid of the problem and the customer senses that. Sorry, it ain't that easy. Don't, for a minute, mistake giving a refund, for resolution. It is not. That guest is an intelligent person with a legitimate complaint and does not deserve such a perfunctory, robotic response. Your business will pay the price for such poor management. More than anything your guest wants to be heard.

Let me suggest the following as a good strategy:

- **Acknowledge** your guest's complaint and agree that if the same happened to you, you would be upset too. Never argue.
- **Make all kinds of excuses. JUST KIDDING!** — Never, no matter how great the temptation, make any excuse. It is childish. It is not the guest's responsibility if your cook has family problems, if someone called in sick or a staff member misread an order. Your guest does not want an excuse, she wants action!
- **Listen** well and understand what your guest is saying. In most cases your guest just wants to be heard and after you listen patiently and sincerely empathize, she will calm down. Usually this is a good sign that resolution is just around the corner.
- **Act** — If it is obvious what will remedy the situation,

then for God's sake get busy doing it right away. If it is not so obvious, ask your guest how she would like for you to handle the problem, and then go above and beyond her expectation. Perhaps buy dessert, or comp the meal and invite them back to dine again on you. You are only out the cost of the food, but you build goodwill this way.

It doesn't matter whether the guest is right or wrong—you should not even think that way. Your guest is upset, and if you plan to stay in the restaurant business, you need to fix the problem. If she is a repeat offender, you will know it (a repeat offender is a guy or gal who wants a free meal and is willing to make a scene to get one. If you are not careful, they will get you again and again). Also note whether this is a one-time complaint or a recurring one. If this is a recurring complaint of a similar type, it may be one particular employee who needs re-training in a certain area, or you may have to address a systemic failure; somewhere you or your employees are not executing and corrective action is needed.

Good service does not happen by accident. It takes serious commitment as well as intensive and ongoing training to create a culture of hospitality, but it is so rewarding. You only get into this business if you love people and want to entertain them, and when your guests leave happy and full, you have received the accolade you came here for (and hopefully a little change too!). Well, that brings us to part three of the Big Three.

Cleanliness:

Cleanliness is next to Godliness—John Wesley

Well, old John must have spent some time in the restaurant business because that is surely Gospel to us in the business. Oh, yeah, if you don't get this one right, you're gonna get religion real quick! This is the last of the Big Three, but again, it is equally as important as the others. No one is going to frequent your restaurant if it is always a mess, it's just that simple. I look around your restaurant and see a mess and my perception is that if this is what you are allowing me to see, I can only imagine the areas that I can't see, specifically, the area where my food is prepared. No thank you, I'll take my business elsewhere. Like quality food and quality service, quality cleanliness is a 24/7 proposition. It never ends. Systems need to be in place and followed to a T. Restaurants across this nation are plastered with signs that read "**Clean as You Go,**" which is self explanatory and really makes the task easy when it is done. In your restaurant you will be responsible for the cleaning protocol. You will set systems for back of the house and incorporated in this plan should be HACCP, which assists with food safety and cleanliness.

You might develop a schedule similar to the following:

Each morning as you arrive at your restaurant make mental notes of anything you might see in the way of trash on your parking lot, write it down and as soon as you can have an employee take care of it. Everything about your approach is important because these things fall in the customer's view. In this business you need to learn to view things from the customer's point of view.

Here are the items you absolutely must take care of daily:

- The single most important act of cleaning in every restaurant. The single most important factor in all of food safety. The thing that I, and all experienced food handlers preach day in and day out, is to **wash hands frequently** and dry them using only single-use paper towels. Our hands are the single greatest cross-contaminators of food.
- Work surfaces and utensils need to be cleaned and sanitized routinely throughout the day. Dishes and silverware must be washed continuously throughout the day.
- Entrance foyer, service counters, service area, soda fountains, dining room tables and chairs must be sparkling clean and smell fresh all of the time because these are the areas where your guests forms their judgment of whether or not to return to your establishment.
- Floors in kitchen, service area and dining room should

be swept and mopped throughout the day as needed. A thorough sweep and mop should always be conducted after close to return everything to new. Remember that "Wet Floor" sign!

- You should clean and sanitize bathrooms every morning and then spot check throughout the day. Also check paper supplies in the morning and at shift change.
- Schedule to detail clean your storage area, walk-in cooler and freezer at least twice a week. In the cooler make sure to get underneath any racks or shelves as that is where blood and food particles spill and harbor dangerous pathogens. Be careful while cleaning coolers not to splash any cleaning chemicals onto food items.

Here is your first cleanliness quiz: What is the difference between clean and sanitary? Answer: clean is free of the visible dirt, sanitary is free of the invisible stuff. When we clean we use warm soapy water and a fresh linen towel and that removes visible dirt, grease and grime build-up; when we sanitize, we use cold water with sanitizer solution. Sanitizer kills living microbes such as E-Coli and Salmonella. Always wash and sanitize all utensils after every use.

Above I spoke about the importance of having standards and making things measurable. By having a quantifiable or measurable standard, you can easily and quickly ascertain whether or not you are meeting that standard and then take corrective action. Remember, I stressed setting measurable standards in Quality Food, Quality Service and Quality Cleanliness and now you are beginning to see why.

Look at the three cases presented here:

1. The standard is 3 ounces per regular order of fries and you have measured an actual weight of 5.5 ounces on average for every order going out.
2. The standard is a smile, greeting, an introduction and a 60-second time for the guest to receive his or her food at the counter. When you measured there was a

smile and greeting, but no introduction and the food took over four minutes to be served.

3. The standard is that the foyer and all service counters are to be kept spotless and bathrooms are to stay clean and sanitized and smell fresh. When you measured, you found the service counters messy, and the bathrooms looked as if they hadn't been cleaned in days.

In each case above you see a variance from your preset standard. It is easily identifiable and easily remedied. To take corrective action in most cases it is important to have a refresher training course for the whole department.

The best tool for reviewing that your Q, S & C standards are being met is through a good Q, S & C operations inspection form. The way an operations inspection form works is it lists each item with some detail of the standard and gives it a maximum possible point value. You then measure actual performance against the standard and give it a point value. An example follows:

	Possible	Actual	Score:	Notes:
Product Temperature	5	5		All temperatures up to standard
Product Portioning	5	2		Over portioning of French fries noted
Product Appearance	5	5		All product appearance up to standard
	15	**12**	**80%**	

In the product quality example above, product temperature has a maximum possible point value of 5 points, and, after reviewing product temperatures, you found that they met the standard and gave the maximum point value. Upon weighing the regular orders of French fries, you found that, on average, they weighed 5.5 ounces, which was over your standard by 2.5 ounces; however, portioning on all other products was right on, so you only deducted 3 points from the possible 5 points for the over-portioning of fries (over-portioning costs big $$$). Finally, all product appearance was up-to-snuff, so you assigned maximum possible points again. All *possible* points are totaled and all *actual* points are totaled. Dividing actual points by possible points gives you your score, stated as a percentage and you will have a corresponding letter grade. For example, the food quality score above would equal a low C in my restaurants.

A good Q S & C evaluation will look in depth at all of these areas and when it is completed the score is totaled and a grade is given. This is the most fantastic way to say "great job" where applicable and to take corrective action where needed. The Q S & C form is a great motivator and by having preset standards, you take the guess work out of the equation. Also it takes the "personal" aspect out of the equation. No one can say that you are "picking on me." Either the standard is met, or it is not. It is very simple. See the next example.

Next, we explore the service section of your Q S & C inspection:

	Possible	Actual	Score:	Notes:
Smile and greeting	4	4		Smile and greeting were great!
Introduction	2	0		No introduction
60 Second service time	5	0		Food took over 4 minutes
	11	4	36%	

This example is for illustrative purposes only and it is for a single occurrence. When you do your inspection, you will measure multiple occurrences and it is doubtful that you will ever see a score like 36%, but look at that! You can see in black and white where you are doing well and where you need to improve. There is nothing subjective about it. This is your report card. This is one of the most important maintenance tasks you as owner or manager can do.

Finally, we take a look at the cleanliness section:

	Possible	Actual	Score:	Notes:
Entranceway/Foyer	3	3		Foyer clean
Service Counter	2	0		Drink stains, used napkins on service counter.
Bathrooms: Clean & Sanitized	5	0		Bathrooms dirty and don't smell fresh
	10	3	30%	

Again, this example is for illustrative purposes only and it is for a single occurrence. When you do your inspection, it will be for numerous items and a number of occurrences and it is doubtful you will see scores like these, although it can happen.

At the conclusion of your inspection you have a snapshot of operations and you will have copious notes on items that need addressing. Now is the time to formulate a plan of action. I would recommend you first coordinate with your leaders or managers or whoever it is that helps you run things and develop your strategy. Schedule a team meeting and perhaps have "breakout" sessions where you take that part of staff responsible for service (and front of the house cleanliness) and your kitchen manager takes the kitchen staff responsible for correct portion sizes, etc. Each addresses the things that went right about the inspection and the things that need to be brought up to speed. Always do these sessions with all of the relevant employees, so that everyone gets the same message.

Another area that a good Q S & C inspection addresses is maintenance items that you, as owner or manager, will need to work on. Perhaps it will require the services of a professional or maybe just a can of paint early one morning. Always address maintenance needs as they arise, because this is one area that can get away from you quickly; if a light bulb burns out change it immediately, or before you know it half your restaurant will be dark; if your baseboard is separating from the wall, repair that immediately. These things influence guests' and employees' subconscious perceptions about you and your business and can undermine your efforts in other areas. Stay on top of maintenance at all times.

There is your introduction to the Big Three. We started the chapter by suggesting that we set standards and make them measurable and now, as we close this chapter, it should make a little more sense. Also at www.cookingwithgas.net we have Q S & C inspection forms that you can easily modify to work in your restaurant. These forms are Excel spreadsheets and calculate all scores for you, so log on now! This is one more tool you can add to your growing kit of tools that make your life as a restaurateur better and improve your guests' experience!

Chapter 10

Risk Management

Often, when asked what I do, I half-jokingly say that the most important thing I do is risk management. Actually, it's the second most important thing I do. I operate successful businesses and, to do that, the most important thing I do is find and train good people, which makes my job as risk manager a whole lot easier. The next most important thing I do is provide a safe environment for both employees and guests (risk management). I work each day to engineer risk out of the businesses I own, and you should, too. In part that is done by hiring the right people in the first place, but you have got to be vigilant at all times. If something doesn't look right, do something about it—now.

So what is risk management? Well, like all good management, it involves planning. Risk management is first about identifying areas of vulnerability to your business, then planning ways to reduce or eliminate loss related to those vulnerabilities. If you are an e-business, and conduct transactions online, you are vulnerable in many ways. Your risk manager would have you install the latest firewall, the best method for encryption, etc., to minimize your and your customers' vulnerability and possible loss. In the restaurant business we face many areas of vulnerability.

Here are just a few:
- Slips and falls —The greatest vulnerability and the most common form of loss in our business.

- Burns and cuts.
- Food borne illness (food safety).
- Wrongful termination.
- Discrimination.
- Violations of laws governing the employment of minors.
- Non-compliance with state and federal requirements for proper record keeping and retention.
- Robbery.
- Sexual harassment.
- Risk to property from fire, weather, and other Acts of God.

The list above outlines some, not all, of our vulnerabilities; they fall into three broad areas that may overlap at times.

1. **Environmental accident.** Numbers 1 and 2. Slips, falls, cuts and burns are all common to the restaurant business. Slips and falls are the single greatest source of liability and loss to the restaurant owner. The most important factor in all of these is set policies and procedures followed by training and constantly stressing safety on the job. It starts in orientation and should follow each employee throughout his or her time with you. In the restaurant setting, tile floors of any type, even quarry or those with a top coat of grit, eventually become slick. Require every employee to wear slip-resistant shoes and, in addition, provide non-skid mats in high traffic areas. They aren't cheap, but they cost a lot less than one slip and fall. I cover every tile walking surface with them; not the whole floor, just the walkways, and we always clean the mats daily. The shoes and mats are both available through your linen supplier or a company called Shoes for Crews. Burns and cuts can be avoided by keeping certain routines and doing it the same each time and no horseplay on the job. Knives and cutting machines should be treated with great respect. Have your employees take great care when disassembling and

reassembling your cutting machine. Also, never put sharp knives in soapy water. The next guy won't see it when he plunges his hand down into that water and will get a nice cut because of someone else's stupidity. A few steps taken by you will reduce a great majority of risk in these areas. Finally, never open the doors until you are adequately insured. Proper insurance is an important part of your risk management portfolio. For these types of accidents and all accidents where an employee is injured on the job, you need to have worker's compensation insurance, which is required by law in most states and is provided by any reputable insurance company. Worker's comp is linked to your payroll and the fewer claims you have the better your rating. The better your rating, obviously, the better your rates. So, it pays to be safe. For accidents involving guests you will need to carry general liability insurance (GL). If an accident occurs on your property which causes injury to a person or damage to property and you are found liable, expect to owe some damages. This is what GL is for. Always do all in your power to create safe environments for employees and guests because it is the right thing to do, but also because many jurisdictions are very favorable to the plaintiff, and in that situation, the onus is upon you to show that you have done everything you possibly could to mitigate danger. All the plaintiff has to do is sit there and look pitiful, with his arm in a sling and a quiver upon his lip, all the while being coached by his attorney and it's a sure bet he's gonna win.

One quick story here will suffice. We own a multiple-unit franchise in a midsize town in south Louisiana. Years ago I was sued by a claimant who claimed our coleslaw made him ill. In his deposition he stated that he purchased the offending coleslaw in one of our restaurants on the south side of town, on a certain day, at a certain time, during a specific time of year, etc., etc. all very detailed and specific. It was a bogus claim and everyone knew it. The insurance company offered him $3,500 to settle out of court. At that time, it was cheaper for the insurance company to "pay off," rather than to fight every claim in court, particularly courts in the area where I live. Now Louisiana tort laws have changed to make it harder for claimants, and insurance companies don't automatically pay. But I digress, back to the story. The claimant declined the $3,500 because he knew he would have better luck before the judge.

In court, his story was completely different from his deposition. Different restaurant, the one on the north side of town, different day, different time—you name it. Nothing in his court appearance agreed with what was already on record in his deposition. But, you guessed it, the judge still found in his behalf. My jaw was on my chest. I couldn't believe it. All I could do was shake my head.

There was one bit of poetic justice, though, a little silver lining if you will. The judge awarded the claimant one half what the insurance company had offered in the first place: exactly $1,750, and I suppose his attorney took most of that. I had a good laugh, but we both went away losers that day; sort of.

2. **Management Practices** —Numbers 3 through 8 above fall under the heading of management practices, meaning they are directly influenced by management. There are local, state and federal guidelines for employment practices, such as how and when you may terminate an employee, requirements for paperwork and its retention, laws governing the hours which a minor employee may work during the school year. You will need to familiarize yourself with local and state ordinances. Start and keep a folder on every employee. In that folder include the employee's application, W-4, State-4, I-9 form, any in-house forms you require, and any written documentation, such as performance appraisals or write-ups pertaining to that employee If your employee is a minor, you will need a work permit, which is issued either by the school or the school board in your town. These forms are required by law and the

penalties can be steep. In the case of the I-9 form any person hired after November 6, 1986 is required to have an I-9 form on file with his or her employer. This form requires identification; its purpose is to ensure that you don't hire an illegal alien. Many employers don't even know of the existence of this form, yet the Justice Department may review them at any time and will give you a 3-day notice. The law provides for fines from $100 to $1,000 per missing or improper I-9 form.

Discrimination is defined as unfair or unlawful treatment of a person belonging to a protected class, as compared to your treatment of others not belonging to a protected class. The protected classes are: race, color, sex, religion, national origin, age, or disability. You must know what constitutes unfair or unlawful treatment, and you need to understand the ways you are required by law to accommodate the protected classes. In most cases, if you're complying with the federal requirements, you will also be complying with the local requirements, but it does pay to know. Penalties can be steep for non-compliance and the old saying holds true here: Ignorance of the law is no excuse. Trust me, I know. I've been there, paid that fine and that's why I am writing this book. Here's another story to illustrate: an applicant once applied for job as a cook with one of our restaurants and, after being offered a job, demanded that she be allowed to wear a dress, for religious purposes. Sorry, but a dress as a cook in this restaurant where you have to filter 340 degree grease twice a day down on your hands and knees, well, a dress just ain't getting it; it was just too dangerous. I told the manager that the applicant would have to wear pants, which is our uniform policy anyway.

That cost me $500.

She filed with the EEOC claiming that I had discriminated against her for religious reasons. That was it—cut and dry. My only goal was to protect a prospective employee from getting burned, but, instead, I was the one who got burned. They slapped the $500 fine on me, pronto. They told me I needed to accommodate her. We did, and when her first day of work rolled around (after we paid the fine), she was nowhere to be seen, and we never heard from her again. Fortunately, this was the only woman who ever made that demand. I would have a real problem with that particular accommodation because by granting it, I have an increased risk of injury on the job. The funny thing is that the EEOC did not care about that risk to the employee. I wondered whether the EEOC's motivation was to protect that person or penalize an employer. This is a blood sport. The crosshairs are on you, and you are getting shot at with real bullets. You had better have the stomach for it. Get some familiarity with those protected classes and what it takes to accommodate them. Pay close attention to the Americans with Disabilities Act. It governs many aspects of our business. For example, if you are building out a site, your restrooms will have to be ADA compliant. You will also need a ramp at or near your entranceway and your door will need to be wide enough to accommodate a wheelchair. Your contractor should be informed of current requirements, but double check just to make sure.

Familiarize yourself with the laws governing the employment of minors, particularly during the school year and obey them. Violations of these laws also carry steep fines that can't be avoided. We opened a new restaurant a few years ago and in our second month, while we were crazy busy, the state Department of Labor agent walked in and proceeded to check our payroll records. We had 72 violations of minors working more than five hours without a break. This after I had specifically trained the managers to ensure that minors took their break at the appropriate time, but again, we were brand new and outrageously busy, so I didn't go hard on them. We were given a warning and we had one month to straighten it out. She came back one month later, and wouldn't you know it...we had one kid who had worked 5 hours and 9 minutes before she took a break, so she was nine minutes over the limit. The fine: $9,000. With that one violation, the 72 previous violations were reactivated. They suspended $8,500 of it (some of you caught that—another $500 fine. It seems to be a theme, like a recurring nightmare).

Then I had to deal with a mediator in our state capitol, who "helped" me by "reducing" my fine; now I have to appease this state employee ensconced safely in an office somewhere in our state capitol, far removed from the trenches where I fight every day. He acted like *he* was doing *me* a favor because I only have to pay $500 but he holds the cards. He makes me write a report on a program, to be developed by me, outlining the numerous steps I would take to make sure that this never happened again. Remember how you got punished in grade school and had to write "I will not do such and such again" 50 times? Well, it was sort of like that. I then had each of my managers sign it so that I could fax it to my new best friend. The form went into each of their folders. It was either that or, I could go to court and fight the $500 fine, but if I lost, I would have to pay the $9,000. He had me over a barrel and he knew it; I paid the $500, wrote the report and that was that, but it was a supremely frustrating experience and took an inordinate amount of time I would have otherwise devoted to operations.

I tell you these stories to impress upon you the gravity of business. The restaurant business is not all fun and games. It is sometimes life and death. Literally.

In most cases robbery of restaurants is an impulse thing. Guy comes in to buy a sandwich, sees the cash drawer over-flowing with ten and twenty dollar bills and decides to help himself. Management must always train staff to keep register drawers drawn down; in other words, siphon off the tens and twenties and keep just fives and ones so that the drawer is not a magnet for an impulse grab. Install mini safes below your counter and put all bills larger that $5 in that safe. In the event you are robbed always train staff to remain calm and to cooperate with the robber. If he gets nervous, things could get ugly real quick. Never, under any circumstances, ever allow your back door to be opened after sunset. Stories abound of horrific crimes that happened because back doors were opened at night. Those crimes often involve a disgruntled former employee usually working with a couple of friends. He knows your habits, knows exactly where whatever it is he wants is, and finally, he has a grudge, which makes him dangerous and sometimes even lethal. While we have never been robbed through the back door, over the years we have been robbed a few times. Once involving a gun, and I can tell you that was scary. Here again, the manager had not followed proper procedure and she could have paid with her life for that violation.

Late one night, after closing, my manager locked up her restaurant and headed across the parking lot to her car. That's the violation right there. All personnel are required to move their cars to the front of the restaurant at some point in the evening while we are still open, which she had failed to do. Anyway, she's approaching her car and a masked guy jumps out of his hiding spot and rushes her with a gun. He marches her back into the restaurant at gun point where she disarms the alarm system, putting in the panic code[7], God bless her, just like she had been trained, all the while being cursed and pistol-whipped across the back of her head by this savage beast cretin crazed on crack cocaine, but the alarm system did not disarm. He ordered her to not worry about it and open the safe. She was so nervous and shaking so badly, not to mention bleeding and dazed, that it took four tries before she could get the safe open. More pistol whipping. More cursing. Finally, she gets it open and with all the cash stuffed in his coat pockets, he flees. While it probably seemed like an eternity, maybe a minute and a half had elapsed since she had opened the front door. These things happen very quickly. She tries the phone, but the phone line had been seized by the alarm system when she put in her duress code. The police never came. After the robber fled, she disarmed the system with her regular code and then made seven more attempts with the duress code. Meanwhile, an employee who had gotten off work and left just before the manager had witnessed the guy rushing the manager and forcing her back to the restaurant. He fled and ran a couple of blocks, knocked on a stranger's door, and convinced him to call the police to the restaurant. Eventually, that call brought the police. Needless to say, everything else is secondary when we are talking about the possible loss of life. I got there at about 12:30 am and I can tell you, this was one traumatic evening. You want to know what happened with the alarm company, don't you? Why they never dispatched the police? Well, let me tell you, so did I, and that company heard from me, both that night and the following days—big time. We could have lost a life because of their negligence. Okay, long story short, after a thorough investigation this is what we found: We had recently torn down and rebuilt that restaurant. So everything in it was new. When our alarm company installed the new alarm system, they left the duress code on the factory default setting, instead of reprogramming it with our unique duress code. So, then, my question to them was that if it wasn't our duress code that the manager first put in, but obviously a wrong code, why didn't that set off an alert? To which they responded, "Well, yes, but then she put the correct code." "Okay", I countered, "but then she followed it with seven more incorrect entries in quick succession. Didn't that seem just a little strange?" They had no answer. They had dropped the ball big time, but so had I. I had not ensured that the correct code was reprogrammed; you have to try to think of everything all of the time, and I had never even given it a thought. I had just assumed and you know what happens when you ass u me! This is what you call experience. You can be sure I'll never let that one happen again!

The alarm company repaid all our losses, but this whole terrifying experience may have been avoided if my manager had just followed procedures and parked up front and been more alert, as I stress with everyone, all of the time. I have some of the best managers in the business, but they are human. We humans make mistakes. We constantly train and retrain; we constantly look for our weak areas, for we know that the arrow will always find that one exposed spot, that one vulnerable area (see the story of Achilles in chapter titled Lagniappe). The police never caught that guy, but the management and team pieced together that he was somehow connected to an employee we had recently fired. When it was all over, it wasn't hard for me to make the argument to all of my managers about the importance of following procedures to the letter. I got some pretty good mileage out of that incident.

Overall, you will never reduce the possibility of robbery to zero, but you can surely improve your odds by developing good safety habits and constantly looking for your weak areas. Be discreet as you leave your restaurant to make your daily deposit. Park your car as near to your door as possible and try to conceal that bright blue or purple bank deposit bag. The bad guy knows what that is. Don't draw attention to yourself.

Install a security system with panic alerts at your POS system. Usually they install a button in a convenient location just beneath the counter. Also, there are fobs that can be worn like a necklace around the neck. These systems require routine maintenance and checks to ensure that they are working properly and constant training/awareness of your unique duress code if you have one. Obviously, if any changes are made to the system, make sure all proper codes have been reprogrammed. Think safety all of the time. Are you getting' it? *NYCWG!*

Sexual harassment is a subject about which you should make yourself and all your managers fully knowledgeable. Here is a brief description: Any circumstance of a sexual nature that makes an employee feel his or her job may be in jeopardy, in any way, could be found to constitute sexual harassment. It may be perpetrated by a man or woman upon any other man or woman. The victim will lodge a complaint with management and call the Equal Employment Opportunity Commission (EEOC). Whenever disciplining someone of the opposite sex, always do so with another manager as witness. Sexual harassment needs to be taken seriously and investigated vigorously. Remember Delila. Have a zero tolerance policy for sexual harassment.

Food safety is another topic that falls under the umbrella of management practices. This is definitely an area of vulnerability to us as food service operators and we discussed it in the previous chapter titled Q S & C. You, or a member of your management, will have to take a food sanitation course and be certified. It is now required in most areas. Contact your local board of health or log on to the National Restaurant Association to find out the requirements in your area. Log on to www.cookingwithgas.net for the link to the National Restaurant Association.

3. **Acts of God** — These are the ones you have no control over. If you live in the Great Plains states, you may, from time to time, have to deal with tornadoes. If you live in the Gulf Coast states, it's hurricanes. The West Coast has earthquakes, mudslides and wildfires. Just about every area has some unpredictable force of nature that ain't in the plans. That's what insurance is for! Adequate coverage for these things is critical to weathering the storms, literally, that nature can throw your way.

Insurance is one of those necessary evils you hope you never need and you probably won't. But when you do, it's usually big and then you thank God you made those payments on time. Trust me, I know. Be smart and shop it. Always get several quotes and only from reputable vendors. Cover as many eventualities as you can afford and <u>always</u> make sure you have "Business Interruption" also known as "Loss of Income" coverage, by whatever name it is called, make sure you have it. Business interruption insurance covers a portion of your on-going expenses like rent and lost income should you be out of commission for a while. Louisiana had a very active hurricane season in 2005 and our restaurants were down for three weeks. I thank God we had business interruption insurance. Many, many businesses weren't able to recover because of inadequate insurance coverage. If you are anywhere close to a flood zone, have proper flood coverage. Ask about wind-driven and rising water and ensure that you insure for both if you can.

Risk management is about identifying areas of vulnerability and protecting your company from losses in those areas. With 13 restaurants operating 363 days a year, we have done very well over the years at risk management and guarded against millions of potential losses, but, as you can see, even being on top of our game, sometimes people make mistakes; managers don't follow a set policy they have been trained on; there's an insufficient understanding of federal and state laws; or, just the fact that you are a business and, therefore, a target all put you at risk and create the potential for losses. You must be on your guard 24/7.

At the beginning of this book reasons for business failure were cited, and, if you remember, the number one reason was lack of management knowledge and experience. Hopefully with each chapter you have gotten a better sense of just what good management entails, and I hope by now you see that it may not be as simple as you once thought. Even with years of experience, we face challenges every day. The path is fraught with peril and strewn with the corpses of those who failed.

In my years in this business I have seen it all and I'll say it again: the investment in time and money to do it right is much cheaper than the potential loss from any of the risks I have discussed. Do it right the first time! *NYCWG!*

One last, but very important note: Make it policy, from day one, that should any emergency occur involving your restaurant and the media become involved, no one but you should comment and you should choose your words very carefully. When in doubt just say "no comment while the investigation is ongoing." It is always better to say too little.

Chapter 11

Taxes, Taxes, Taxes

There are two sure things in life: death, and taxes. Death is, by far, the more pleasant of the two. It's true. Preparing and selling great food is sensual and exciting. Talking with my guests, making new friends and making sure they all have a great experience is fun. Building my team up and seeing each one of them grow is rewarding. Doing taxes; well, suffice it to say, I'd rather take a beating. As an employer you will be responsible for various tax withholdings and payment and, as you might imagine, this is not one of the more pleasant aspects of business ownership. I recommend investigating a good payroll service. Interview several in your area, get a reference list and call them. Also, we provide access to a wonderful service that I have used for years. You can find it through www.cookingwithgas.net However, I'm still gonna teach you about taxes because if there is one trap that more first time business owners fall into, early on, than any other, it is this: the temptation to forestall payment of taxes.

The taxes I refer to are:
- Payroll taxes
- Federal and state unemployment taxes
- Sales taxes

Many first time business owners literally have no idea that some of these taxes even exist and are taken completely by surprise by them. Actually, they had some idea of these taxes, but their understanding of the subject can best be described as murky. They never understood the employer's role in their collection and remittance. Even after learning about them, often, at first when cash flow isn't going well, there is a temptation to put off paying these taxes, but you do so at peril to your business. The penalties are swift and sure and can not be avoided. Many businesses have gone under due to delinquent taxes. Word to the wise: pay in a timely fashion. The IRS doesn't play.

The payroll taxes are federal and state income tax, Social Security and Medicare tax (FICA), federal unemployment tax (FUTA) and state unemployment tax (SUTA). The employer withholds the federal income taxes, Social Security and Medicare tax (FICA), matches the SS and Medicare tax and then deposits those sums either semiweekly or monthly depending on the "Look Back" test. The IRS "looks back" at your two previous years of business ending on the last day of the most recent month of June and extending backwards from that last day of June two years to the 1st day of July two plus years ago, so let me rephrase that; the IRS takes the most recent two-year period from July 1st to June 30th. If payroll taxes paid during the two-year look back period were less than $50,000 then you are a monthly depositor. If payroll taxes paid during the look back period were greater than $50,000 then you are a biweekly depositor. The deposit is made by either mailing payment to the IRS, or delivering a check, money order, or cash to a bank or financial institution that is an authorized depository for federal taxes. The employer files quarterly returns using the IRS form 941 Employer's Quarterly Federal Tax Return, due the last day of the month following each quarter: 1st quarter is January to March so returns will be due on April 30th, and so forth: July 31st, October 31st and January 31st.

- Federal income tax is a progressive tax and each employee pays at his "marginal rate" which is determined by his annual income. For these thresholds you may consult the IRS website at www.irs.gov. Also, these thresholds are built into your accounting software.
- State income tax is usually a factor of the federal

tax and its deposit schedule may differ from federal income tax, so you will need to verify that in your state

Currently the factor to withhold is 6.20% for Social Security and 1.45% for Medicare. But here's the catch: In addition to not knowing these taxes even existed, many first time employers also don't realize that you match your employees' Social Security and Medicare tax contribution. It's an additional cost of labor. Here's how it works: If your employee, Suzie Shellmaker, earns $100, you will withhold $6.20 from her paycheck for Social Security taxes and $1.45 for Medicare. Then you match an additional $6.20 in Social Security and $1.45 in Medicare taxes for a grand total of $15.30 (15.30%) that is deposited. Her W-2, which you mail out each January, will only reflect her portion of the contribution. All those years you have worked and you probably never realized your employer was doing the same for you. By the final day of January you must have mailed W-2's from the previous year to every current and former employee. You will the mail IRS a W-3, which is a summary of all your W-2 information, every employee and his or her taxes paid, to the IRS.

Next you have federal unemployment tax and its sibling state unemployment tax. The federal unemployment tax is usually 8/10ths of 1% and is due quarterly. For this tax you use IRS form 940.

Depositing FUTA Tax

When to deposit. Although Form 940 covers a calendar year, you may have to make deposits of the tax before filing the return. Generally, deposit FUTA tax quarterly if your FUTA tax exceeds $500. Determine your FUTA tax for each of the first three quarters by multiplying by .008 that part of the first $7,000 of each employee's annual wages you paid during the quarter. If any part of the amounts paid is exempt from state unemployment tax, you may be required to deposit an amount greater than that determined using the .008 rate. For example, in certain states, wages paid to corporate officers, certain payments of sick pay by unions, and certain fringe benefits are exempt from state unemployment tax.

If your FUTA tax for any of the first three quarters of the year (or the year plus any undeposited amount of $500 or less from any earlier quarter) is over $500, deposit it by the last day of the first month after the end of the quarter. If it is $500 or less, carry it to the next quarter as a deposit is not required. If your FUTA tax for the fourth quarter (plus any undeposited amount from any earlier quarter) is over $500, deposit the entire amount by January 31 of the following year. If it is $500 or less, you can either make a deposit or pay it with your Form 940 by January 31. (If you deposit it by January 31, you may file Form 940 by February 10th.). The deposit due dates are shown in the following chart

If undeposited FUTA tax is over $500 on: Deposit it by

If undeposited FUTA tax is over $500 on:	Deposit it by
March 31	April 30
June 30	July 31
September 30	October 31
December 31	January 31

TIP

If any deposit due date falls on a Saturday, Sunday, or legal holiday, you may deposit on the next business day.

How to deposit. If you choose not to enroll in EFTPS and are not required to use EFTPS (see electronic deposit requirement below), use Form 8109, Tax Deposit Coupon, when you make each tax deposit.

The IRS will pre-enroll you in EFTPS when you apply for an employer identification number (EIN). Follow the instructions in your EIN package to activate your enrollment and begin making your tax deposits. New employers who would like to receive a Federal Tax Deposit (FTD) coupon booklet can call the IRS at 1-800-829-4933. Allow 5 to 6 weeks for delivery. Your state unemployment tax will most likely also be quarterly, but you will need to double check that to be sure.

Yeah, isn't this scintillating and fun! Sort of like a visit to the tribal dentist where they chip your front teeth out with a rock, slowly, with no medication, to groom you for manhood. I'd rather be a sissy!

This is one area I confess to being a lightweight. It's just too much hassle and takes me away from other, far more productive pursuits. A long time ago, I got rid of these problems by hiring a payroll service. To me this service is worth its weight in gold because, among the many services they provide, they calculate these taxes and make the deposits, they do the returns, they take care of all W-2's and W-3's, etc. leaving me free to sell hamburgers, chicken, pizza—whatever. And guess what?! they even do sales taxes! I highly recommend you find a reputable payroll service like the one we have. If you would like the services of our payroll company, log on to www.cookingwithgas. net for more information. Otherwise you will soon need to hire a bookkeeper.

The next item on the hit parade list is sales taxes. You act as a collection agent for your city, county and state. That's how they derive their income. You collect taxes at the time of the sale and then you pay monthly to your city, county and state, usually due no later than the 20th of the following month, so sales taxes for June would be payable by July 20th. Typically you are mailed the forms by the taxing body. In many cases you can do the form online and pay by electronic funds transfer. The tax factor usually has a municipal, county and state component, but every locale is different. Our tax factor here is 8.50%. The county gets 4% and 4.50% goes to the state. Some taxing authorities offer a discount for taxes paid on your cost of goods for the period. Make sure you take any and all available discounts! Redundant words to the wise again: pay your taxes in a timely fashion. You got it. *NYCWG*!

Quickfax

- *Of the two sure things in life, death is by far preferable.*
- *You are responsible for knowing as much as possible about, collecting and remitting: payroll taxes, federal and state unemployment taxes and sales taxes (or pay someone to do it for you).*
- *You match Social Security and Medicare.*

- *Federal and (most) state income taxes are progressive withholding taxes.*
- *FUTA and SUTA you pay.*
- *Payroll taxes are made by either mailing payment to the IRS, or delivering a check, money order, or cash to a bank or financial institution that is an authorized depository for federal taxes.*
- *Sales taxes are remitted to local authorities and state Departments of Revenue.*
- *Pay your taxes in a timely manner.*
- *Log on to www.cookingwithgas.net and let us help!*
- *NYCWG!*

Chapter 12

Strategies for Success

For starters, let your first strategy be to read and internalize everything you read within these pages because this book is written for you to give you every chance for success. After you finish this book, get your hands on as much material as you can about the restaurant business. Read everything. Talk with other restaurateurs and ask lots of questions. Consult your attorney and your CPA before making key decisions. Now let's take a look at other strategies for success.

After ignorance, Delila's failure was a failure to plan, and remember what happens when you fail to plan. Strategy is nothing more than a plan of action and, like all good planning, it takes place in advance of events. Strategy is organized, methodical, steps to accomplish a set of objectives. If you plan to open a restaurant, you must begin a year in advance thinking, asking questions and informing yourself.

You will need a strategy for:

- Site location: Remember to match concept to audience and always be culturally sensitive. Look at traffic, ingress and egress, suitable customer and employee base. Any upcoming infrastructure changes? Possible seizure by eminent domain?
- Organizing your business: do you want to be an LLC or a sub-chapter-s corporation? Figure it out then get busy. As soon as you are done with that, go to the IRS and get your EIN.
- Construction: if you will be building a new site or

improving an existing one. Contact contractors and
get bids. Get clear information on timeframes and you
might consider some type of performance contract
to keep the date of completion and costs in line and
then crack the whip. Check regularly on construction
and follow progress of electrical, plumbing, etc. Stay
in touch with your city and have each department
inspect each phase as it is completed. To inhabit a
building, you will need a certificate of occupancy and
you cannot get a certificate of occupancy until every
inspection is complete. Make sure all equipment will
fit through doorways and around corners. Otherwise,
you may need to leave a wall out until equipment is set
in place.

- Get set up with city and county regulatory bodies as
well as your state Department of Revenue and the
IRS. Be sure to ask plenty of questions.

- Point Of Sale equipment: research this and you may
even find reconditioned POS systems at good prices.
A good POS system is important to your success. If
you are a franchisee, chances are you franchisor has
proprietary equipment for you to use.

- Start shopping insurance. Remember: Business
interruption, liability, worker's comp, fire.

- Advertising: The main mediums for advertising are
TV, radio and newspaper. Advertising is a big chunk
of your budget, but it is a necessary evil. If you know
others in your type of business try to find out what has
worked for them. You have gotta let your prospective
customer know that you are there, but you need to
do pricing first and then decide on the right mix for
you and keep it reasonable. All costs must be held to
a minimum in order to give you time to accumulate
a little cash. Consider a "soft" opening; no advance
advertising. This lets you and your team get things
together and find a rhythm as your business grows
before advertising starts. Often too much advertising

in advance of opening brings business you are not ready for and you send away many unsatisfied customers! That is never a good thing.

- Consider a payroll service, and remember, we have a good one.
- Hiring: You need a timetable for hiring, and timing is everything; you hire too early and you lose a portion in the interim between date of hire and opening; hire too late and you don't have sufficient time for training. Do you have skills (remember, skills are learned, you are not born with them) for hiring and employing people? This is a combination of science and art honed over time; if you have never done it, make sure you read the chapter on Organizing and Influencing.
- Make it your goal to institute good record keeping from the very first day. Track: Daily cash, credit card sales, gift card redemptions, etc. on a daily cash report. Track daily and cumulative sales and labor information on a sales and labor form. Track all food movement through your restaurant and do your inventory weekly; preferably Sunday night. Keep your checkbook up to date daily.
- In the same vein as the previous point, make it your goal to understand and control food and labor costs from the very first day of business.
- Foster a culture of hospitality and service.
- Review of operations: An ongoing part of operations is to grade yourself. This is done through an assessment form and as explained previously, looks at the three critical areas: Quality Food, Quality Service and Quality Cleanliness.
- Continue to learn everything you can about this business. Remember, knowledge is power.

Chapter 13

Lagniappe

Lagniappe is French for *"a little something extra."* And that's what I hope to provide here. I wanted to share these things with you, but couldn't find a place elsewhere in the book to put them. Maybe there is a nugget in here just for you. I hope so!

- Fortune favors the well prepared.
—*Julius Caesar*
- Guest walks into your restaurant and everything is as it should be. He doesn't notice.
- Guest walks into your restaurant and a few little things are amiss; he notices all of it and it impacts his overall experience adversely. Moral: guests are just like spouses. Take care of the little stuff. Do those inspections!
- *"That's not my job."* I hate those words. They make me coil like a snake (and then strike!).
- If you are forming a corporation for the first time, do yourself a favor and pick up a copy of "Roberts Rules of Order" to familiarize yourself with parliamentary procedures. Published in 1896 it is as indispensable and relevant to orderly business meetings today as it was the day it was published.
- Partnerships don't work. It is my opinion, and remember, opinions are worth what you paid for them, but I truly believe that. In general, a partnership

is a terrible way to ruin a great friendship. Successful partnerships are a minority.

- Question: is the customer/guest always right? No. But we always treat him like he is. Now that's empowering! Instead of drilling that old falsehood that the customer is always right into your employees' heads, liberate them with the truth. That creates a win-win-win situation. The guest wins, your employee wins and, finally, you win.

- People are like Mother Nature: at times gentle, warm and nurturing and at other times like the torrents of a wild hurricane. You need to understand and work with people and it won't always be easy.

- Your boss: may not be as smart as you are and if you help him to understand this very important point, you will pay, and I mean dearly.

- Your employees: are probably as smart as or smarter than you and that's a good thing. Always cultivate smart people. Smart people help you and they make you look good.

- Your peers: conniving, manipulating, enemy, back-stabbing, upwardly bound, supportive, partner, loving, friend. At one point or another, your peers will be all of these. 'Nuff said. You get it. (*NYCWG!*)

- Swing for the stands every time. Dance like no one is watching. Live like there is no tomorrow. Yeah right, and if you do that, chances are you will be dog-tired after the third swing, never hit the stands and not worth a crap for the next eight innings. Everyone is watching and if you dance like that you will make a fool out of yourself. There is a tomorrow, but if you lived that way yesterday, you ain't gonna be able to pay the bills today. I'm not recommending that you be a cynic without hope. Be very hopeful, but in a reasonable way. Take your time and be steady and consistent. Do only what you can reasonably handle. Do you follow me? (*NYCWG!*)

- Always praise in public and criticize in private (just be sure you have a witness!).
- Catch people doing things right!
- As owner or manager at times you will be called upon to be one of the following: psychologist, mommy, daddy, teacher, police officer, mediator, judge, care giver, terminator, priest; some times it's easy, sometimes it can be downright difficult. Certain cases require time for reflection; don't make a hasty decision. Present the quandary to your subconscious and then sleep on it.
- Make a spreadsheet with all the telephone numbers you call regularly and post it in your office over the phone. Numbers you might include: vendors and vendor's service departments; example: Coca Cola Corporate and Coca Cola Service, merchant services for your credit cards, key employees, emergency (police, sheriff and fire), maintenance companies such as air conditioner repair, fire extinguishing, grease trap cleaning and trash removal, your pest control service.
- Never manage by memo. Be a hands-on manager or hire one.
- Here's a seed I often plant in my employees' heads: I begin by asking what they currently pay for a quick-service meal, say, burger and fries. About $6 to $7 is usually the answer. *"Okay, how long did you have to work to earn the $6 to $7?"* About an hour is the usual answer. *"Okay, so you literally paid for your meal with One Hour of your Life. An hour that will never be relived and you can never recapture?"* The answer is, *"Yes"*, but now I can see the wheels turning in their little heads. *"Did you get service equal to One Hour of your Life? Was the product a decent value for One Hour of your Life?"* Usually they really have to think about this one. I think you, good reader, can see where I am going with this; I want to make the corollary between my employee and our guest, who is paying for her meal with us with that

same dear, precious Hour of her Life, never to be recaptured. I end by reminding each employee that he should always demand the utmost for each and every cent spent. Often, I try not to actually make the corollary, but rather, pray that my seed germinates and that each employee makes that correlation on his or her own; it's a gamble, but I want people to grow.

- Start easy, save some along the way and finish strong. You win when you finish strong. If you fly out of the gate, you will come in late.
- Sure it's hard. It's gonna be hard doing all or even most of the things in this book, but anything and everything that is worthwhile is hard and that's a good thing. You always appreciate so much more that which you have worked to create. And, in case I haven't made this point quite clear enough, it's a lot cheaper than the alternative.
- Beware the toes you tread upon on the way up that ladder, they just may be attached to the rear end you have to kiss on the way back down.
- In financial negotiations, the guy that mentions an amount first, loses.
- If you are building, or doing a build-out, measure all your kitchen equipment, seating, etc. to make sure that will fit through existing doors and around all corners. We once did a build out and realized, fortunately, in time that the grill and its hood vent would not be able to be brought into the kitchen once the walls were up. We left out a wall and the entire bar until that piece was delivered and installed.
- You can't travel back. The past is gone. The future ain't here yet. You have only this moment; this moment is where you harvest the crops from seed planted yesteryear and is the fertile ground into which you plant the seeds of your tomorrow. Plant wisely!
- Smile; often.
- Live by checklists. Sunday night make a list of things

you would like to accomplish for the week. Each day have a checklist of items that need to be accomplished that day and then do it. PDA's help a bunch!

- Write this quote down. When it comes into your head, write it down. When you remember something, when you have a question, when you have a brilliant idea, write it down. It's hard keeping it all in your head during those busy days and if you don't write it down, you'll forget.
- When your employees take a message make sure they always get: name, time of call and date.
- Read:

The Millionaire Next Door by Thomas J. Stanley & William D. Danko

The Prince by Niccolo Machiavelli

The Art of Worldly Wisdom by Baltasar Gracian

The Art of War by Sun Tzu

The Wall Street Journal

- Definition — Crisis Management: "I couldn't get to that because I was stuck here, working!" When you are trapped on the never-ending spiral of not doing the things you need to do because you are too busy doing things others were supposed to do, it's time for another checkup from the neck up. Something is not right. You, not "them," have fallen short somewhere. You either hired the wrong "them" or are not disciplined enough to control "them" or your business is financially strapped and in its death throes, in which case, pull the plug. Cut your losses and move on to something new. You will be so much happier as a result. I know, I know—the money thing. I don't have an easy answer for that.
- Treat your employees the way you want them to treat your guests. The guest experience is always a reflection of the employee experience.
- We are each like a single grain of sand upon all the beaches of the Earth. And yet we sometimes behave

as if the oceans of the world should bathe only this one grain. The ocean will always bathe all grains equally.

- Make as many means of payment as possible available to your guest. If you are going to accept personal checks, make sure you have a service to verify the funds are available before the guest leaves.

- Keep a stash of inexpensive thermometers on hand in your office and have all staff checking food temperatures regularly.

- Behavior (action) comes from feelings. Feelings are created by thoughts. *You* determine your thoughts. Think about that. (*NYCWG*)

- Know your strengths and weaknesses. Focus your efforts and energy where you are strong.

- The same for your employees. Put your "Aces in their places."

- Avoid, at all costs, handwritten signs. They give the impression of a lack of professionalism. It is quicker, and much nicer, to write that same message using your computer.

- Always have a labeling machine handy.

- The world will know you by what you say of others. What you say about your friends and enemies, says much more about you than it does about them.

- You will want to set up an organized filing system.

Group current employees separately from terminated and keep them both filed alphabetically.

After paying bills, staple the check stub to the invoice and group paid bills by vendor. That way when you need to research a bill from three month ago, you can go right to that vendor's folder and will be able to locate the invoice easily.

- Never, ever allow the back door of your restaurant to be opened after dark.

- Always be wary when you pull onto your parking lot. Move your car as near to the front door as possible before it gets dark and prior to taking your deposit to the bank.

- Always be discreet with deposits. Do not flaunt the blue or red or purple or whatever colored bank bag that contains your deposit; keep it under wraps.
- If you want to make your restaurant GREAT check out the cool stuff at www.cookingwithgas.net.
- I know that I have called them "customers" at times in this book, but get in the habit of thinking of and calling them your "guests." A customer is just another joe walking through your door, but a guest is someone you have invited over for a pleasant experience with you (and your employees) as host; treat them like royalty! Remember: <u>Guest</u> not customer.
- Paraphrase of an old saying: "Don't swallow a camel, yet choke on a flea." It's another way of saying, "don't sweat the small stuff."
- Invest in a safe. Have it bolted down in your office and keep all "drawers" (whatever monies you use to start each) day, plus a change fund of a fixed amount in the safe; make at least two deposits each day religiously. DO NOT let deposits sit and accumulate in the safe. That is a big no-no. Be wary when making a drop in the bank's overnight deposit drawer—look around as you pull onto the bank's parking lot and never make a drop after dark. This means that during the winter months you have to be especially disciplined to get to that bank before sunset.
- Keep a journal in your restaurant and record everything. Particularly unusual weather, power outages (a few hours without power can be a real hit to sales), parades, sporting events or anything that impacts business for the good or bad. A year from now you will wonder why you are up or down so much on the same day this year versus last. Also, it's just fun to look back and see what was going on! Check www.cookingwithgas.net first.
- As you go through time in business, events will happen for which you will need to develop a new policy. Do it

right away and have everyone sign off on it and then add it to your policies and procedures manual. If you don't have a policies and procedures manual, one can be found at www.cookingwithgas.net

- There are workplace posters required by both the United States Department of Labor and your own state's Department of Labor. They must be hung in a conspicuous place in your restaurant. Check www.cookingwithgas.net first.

- At some point toward the end of your first year you will need an off-site storage facility for the records you will have to keep, if at all possible, store your records a couple of inches off of the ground. See our records retention list at the end of this book and online at www.cookingwithgas.net.

- Consider hiring a payroll service. Shop for one with good rates; they will improve your peace of mind tremendously by making your payroll tax deposits, taking care of W-2's and many other payroll related duties. In addition, you might consider leasing your employees. You will find a great payroll service at www.cookingwithgas.net

- Always use clear trash liners and make a habit of spot checking your trash by having an employee lift a bag out of the can so that you can see into it to make sure nothing of value is on its way out of your back door. Things to look for: trays, silverware and food.

- Remember, your managers and employees watch what you watch. If you are not watching anything, well, guess what...

- I like the word "team" better than the word "crew."

- Practice aggressive tax avoidance, but not evasion.

- The ancient Greeks had life figured out and have gifted the world with a myth for every life circumstance. The one I cite here is one that applies often in business; it is the story of Achilles. This is the super-abbreviated version, but I am sure you will see how it applies in our business:

During the time of Achilles, one achieved immortality by being submerged in the river Styx. Achilles' mother wanted to make sure that her son was immortal so she took him to the river Styx. As she submerged his entire body in the river, she held him between her thumb and forefinger by that narrow tendon just above your heel. Consequently, that one tiny spot was not touched by the magic waters of the Styx.

Achilles went on to become Greece's most famous warrior hero; seemingly undefeatable, until, one day in the heat of battle, a wildly flung arrow found its mark. Can you guess where that arrow caught the great work? Stopped the show? That's right. The area left vulnerable—his heel. And so it is in business. The one area you put off, leave undone or figure you'll take care of tomorrow—is where that arrow will catch you.

- Never pay the band before they play.

—*Gypsy Proverb*

- There is a natural tension between front of house (waiters) and back of house (cooks, preps, line men, dishwashers). The back of house perceives that waiters make a whole lot of money for very little work, while they work longer hours under hot and difficult conditions for less. It can get downright explosive at times. Often, waiters make this problem worse by discussing how much they made publicly. Teach your front of house staff to be more aware and sensitive.

- Take some time to study the ideas set forth in this book. Cooking With Gas makes no claim to be the final authority on any subject presented herein, but we have provided you with a broad overview and maybe a few specifics and hopefully you know a little more as you finish this book than you did when you first started. Continue to do your homework as there is no such thing as being over-informed in this business. Check your local public library, or better yet, if you have a college library nearby that would be a great resource for information to further your education.

- Develop some understanding of the Family and Medical Leave Act of 1993. It contains laws regarding leaves of absence that affect you and you need to be informed.

- If you don't have sufficient capital to do this business correctly, I most strongly urge you not to do it. While the restaurant business can be profitable, sometimes wildly so, and fun, it is also grueling, hard, unforgiving; the bullets coming at you are real, the hours early on are unbelievable, even when you follow the principles outlined in this book, employees are difficult, customers are difficult, and if you go into this undercapitalized, after all your blood, sweat and tears, the incredibly hard work and long hours, to go belly-up can be quite a blow both emotionally and financially. Don't do it.

- Set your hot water heater to about 120 to 125 degrees so that hands don't get scalded.

- After you form your corporation or LLC, credit card applications will flood your mailbox. Be very careful in building your corporate credit.

Reader:

In Chapter One I promised I would try to scare you away from this business, but I probably haven't scared you badly enough to give up your dream. You need to know the difficulty that lies ahead of you in a full and honest way and that it is critical that you do things correctly from the start. It always costs a little more to do it right the first time, but not near as much as doing it wrong! Our website, www.cookingwithgas.net, has many resources such as worksheets for honing your skills, a Team Handbook template that you can download and modify to fit your company, wall charts for your in-house training program, inspection forms to do your own inspection on your restaurant, links to secretaries of state and all kinds of cool stuff. We also sell, at very reasonable prices, various spreadsheets, developed by us that help you track your business and analyze trends. Track your labor and food costs and manage those using tools such as weekly inventory sheets and variance reports. I have seen similar programs that cost thousands of dollars and are too difficult to even open let alone operate. Do not be fooled; my products are simple and very reasonably priced and will make all the difference to your operations. What I really want is for you to succeed.

I would like you to know that we stand ready to help you. On staff we have an attorney and CPA to answer questions you may have relating to business. You should arrange for the services of a CPA on a monthly basis to prepare your financial statements if you can afford it; if not, then definitely for your annual tax return. We retain the services of just such a firm if you should have the need. Keep good records to make you CPA's work easier and it will cost less. If your paperwork is a jumbled mess, it will take your CPA longer to sort it out, resulting in higher costs to you. Also you should contract the services of a good attorney for further understanding of laws governing your business. Prior to making any big decision, always consult relevant professionals.

I am available to you for consulting services at any step in your process. Also we have a creative department that can assist you with logo or brand development, menu development and a host of other services. If you like the look of our book and website, our creative department can do similar things for you.

We at Cooking With Gas, LLC hope you enjoyed this book and we look forward to hearing from you.

Note: Delila means "poor." Look it up. I don't want you to be Delila.

Glossary

Accrual basis —Revenue is recorded in the books when the sale is made regardless of whether you received any cash or not. Expense is recorded when you received that good or service regardless of whether you spent cash or not.

Annual Report —There are two annual reports not to be confused with one another. One is given by a corporation to its stockholders outlining the previous year's business including the financial statements, etc. The second annual report, and the one we are more concerned with for our purpose, is a yearly filing, not required in all states, that provides updated information on owners and lets the state know that your corporation/LLC is still a viable entity.

Asset —Items of value that you own. There are tangible assets such as cash, real property, and securities, and there are intangibles such as goodwill, patents or copyrights.

Balance Sheet —The financial statement that shows the equality of a company's assets (things the company owns) and its liabilities (claims by other on the things company owns) plus owners equity.

Beginning Cash —Cash position at the beginning of a fiscal cycle.

Business Plan —A description of your products or services, description of key personnel and their talents and role in proposed business, analysis of your market, analysis of your competition, sales forecasts, growth forecasts for five years, what external financing will be required. This is an important tool to focus your vision and to win over prospective investors.

Cash Basis —Revenue is recorded when you receive cash and expenses are recorded when you spend cash.

Cash Disbursements — Line item on the cash flow statement indicating cash payments.

Cash Flow Statement — Report detailing cash activities for a period. Beginning cash plus all cash received during the period from sales and financing activities less cash paid out equals net cash flow.

Certificate of Occupancy — Upon completion of all inspections by the various regulatory departments within your municipalities' government, you are issued your CO which grants you the right to occupy the premises.

Controlling Function — One of the four functions of management. The process of comparing actual performance with pre-set standards and taking corrective action where necessary.

Corporate Shield — Protects the personal assets of shareholders of a corporation.

Corporation — A type of business organization granted by each state and owned by shareholder(s). Recognized as a separate legal entity, with all rights appertaining to same.

Cost of Goods — Line item of the income statement showing the cost of inventory items purchased during a given period and used for resale.

CPA — Certified Public Accountant.

Demographics — The race, age, income level, education, occupation and other qualities used for market targeting.

Depreciation — The reduction in value of a capital asset and its corresponding expense charged against the revenues of a company on the income statement. Depreciation considers the salvage or scrap value of an asset and subtracts that from the assets initial value. The difference is spread over periods as an expense to business using different formulas. The most common formula is "Straight Line" Depreciation.

Discrimination — Defined as unfair or unlawful treatment of a person belonging to a protected class as compared to your treatment of others not belonging to a protected class. The protected classes are: race, color, sex, religion, national origin, age, or disability

Double Taxation — Corporations pay tax on profits. When those after-tax profits are then distributed to shareholders in the form dividends, that shareholder is taxed on the dividend as it comes to him which means that the same money has been taxed twice. This is one reason many entrepreneurs choose the Limited Liability Company (LLC) or Sub chapter-s corporation form of business organization.

Egress — Point of exit, the pathway to exit. You want for your egress to be unobstructed.

Employer Identification Number (EIN) — A unique identification number granted by the Internal Revenue Service to a company and is used to identify that company. Similar to the Social Security Number for Americans.

Expenses — Operating and administrative costs incurred in the normal operation and maintenance of a business to generate revenue.

Franchise — A contractual agreement between franchisor, who grants certain legal rights including name usage to a franchisee, who agrees to abide by the terms of the agreement.

Federal Income Tax — A progressive tax, with each employee paying at his/her "marginal rate" as determined by annual income

Federal Unemployment Tax (FUTA)

Forms/File Retention — Different forms are required by law to be held by you for prescribed periods of time. See file retention addendum.

HACCP (Hazard Analysis and Critical Control Points) — A systematic approach to the prevention of food contamination by any or all of the three hazards to food safety during the flow of food from production through the restaurant until it is served to a guest. The three hazards to food safety are: physical hazard, biological hazard and chemical hazard

Human Resource Administration — Perform various staffing related internal functions.

Human Resource Planning — Anticipate your future needs for employees.

General Liability Insurance — A form of insurance designed to protect owners of businesses from a variety of liability exposures. These exposures could include liability arising from accidents resulting from the premises or the operations of insured, products sold by the insured, operations completed by the insured.

Income Statement —Also known as the P & L statement, this statement shows all revenues from operations and all expenses generated earning those revenues. Revenue minus expenses equals net income aka profit.

Influencing (Leading) —The ability to **motivate** others.

Ingress —Point of entry, the pathway to entry. You want your ingress to be unobstructed.

IRS form SS-4 —The IRS form used to apply for your Employer Identification Number.

Job analysis —Defining the job duties and then determining the skills required to perform those duties.

Liability —In accounting terms it is any claim on assets. In business terms, it implies exposure to risk.

Limited Liability Company —A type of business organization granted by each state and owned by its members. A legal entity that may engage in business, build credit. The LLC confers many of the same protections of personal assets as the corporation, while providing the favorable tax treatment of partnerships.

Management —Coordination of company resources (personnel, money and equipment) to achieve the stated mission and goals of the company.

Medicare Tax —Employer deducts these taxes from each wage payment.

Mission Statement —A brief (one to five sentences) philosophical statement outlining the founder's core beliefs and values directly pertaining to his/her business and its operation. It is the mold into which you pour your ideas. Stay true to it and your company will resemble it. See mission statement addendum.

Morale —The capacity of a person or group to have positive feelings for and believe in an organization and its goals.

Motivation —The willingness to put forth effort in pursuit of organization goals.

Net Cash Flow —Beginning cash plus all cash received during the period from sales and financing activities less cash paid out equals net cash flow.

Net Income —Also known as profit, this is the difference between all revenues from operations and all expenses incurred to generate that revenue during a specific period.

NYCWG! — Now You're Cooking With Gas!

Organizational Culture —A system of shared values, beliefs, customs and behavioral patterns within an organization.

Organizing —The process of recruiting, hiring, orienting and training staff.

Owner's Equity —Assets minus liabilities equal owner's equity.

Performance Appraisal —Evaluate performance and progress on the job.

Planning —The number one function of management. It is defined as: to determine, in advance, methods and actions to be taken to achieve stated goals and objectives.

Positive Reinforcement —The administration of positive consequences for desirable behavior tends to increase the likelihood of future desirable behavior in a similar setting. Translation: treat people well when they do a job you are happy with and they will likely duplicate that performance under similar circumstances.

Product Yield —Denotes the number of portions we get from a case or unit of something; for example a bag of mashed potato mix will yield 50 small servings.

Productivity —The yield on human labor; the number, in sales dollars, produced per hour of labor.

Profit and Loss (P & L) Statement —Same as income statement.

Projections —An estimate of future sales based upon recent sales.

Q, S & C —Quality Product, Quality Service and Quality Cleanliness. The "Big Three."

Recruiting —To attract qualified applicants.

Sales Mix —The percentage of total sales for each menu item. It is calculated by dividing sales of that item by total sales. Example: Hamburger sales $8,400. Total sales $20,000. Hamburger is 42% of the mix.

S-Corporation —A designation granted by the IRS that provides a more favorable tax treatment for small businesses than a c-corporation. An eligible domestic corporation can avoid double taxation (once to the corporation and again to the shareholders) by electing to be treated as an s-corporation. Generally, an s-corporation is exempt from federal income tax other than tax on certain capital gains and passive income. On their tax returns, the s-corporation's shareholders include their share of the corporation's separately stated items of income, deduction, loss, and credit, and their share of nonseparately stated income or loss.

Sales Yield —A measure of recent performance that is useful for planning. Sales for a period divided by the number of items used for the same period equals the sales yield.

Sanitary — Indicates free of all invisible pathogens and microbes.

Selection — Choosing the employee who possesses the skills required to perform the tasks defined in job analysis or definition.

Sexual Harassment —Any circumstance of a sexual nature that makes an employee feel his or her job may be in jeopardy, in any way, could be found to constitute sexual harassment. It may be perpetrated by a man or woman upon any other man or woman. The victim will lodge a complaint with management and call the Equal Employment Opportunity Commission (EEOC).

Shrinkage — Loss caused by employee waste and theft.

Social Security —The employer deducts these taxes from each wage payment. Social Security coverage provides retirement benefits.

State Income Tax —An income tax imposed by most states. Most states utilize the progressive tax structure similar to the federal code. A few states impose no state income tax.

State Unemployment Tax (SUTA) —Like FUTA, this is a payroll related tax paid by the employer. Generally, your SUTA tax rate is based on the amount of unemployment claims that are filed by employees you have terminated. When your business is new, your SUTA tax rate starts at the maximum and declines if you build a history of few claims.

Synergy —The working together of two or more people that produces output greater than the sum of their individual outputs. Teamwork produces synergy.

Team Meetings —An important team maintenance activity. This is the time to talk about all the things that are going right and address areas where the team has failed to meet standards. Also a great time to plan upcoming specials and recognize and reward outstanding performance.

Team —A small group of people with complimentary skills, who work together to achieve a common purpose for which they hold themselves collectively accountable.

Temperature Danger Zone —41 to 140 degrees.

Training —Once an employee is selected, he or she is trained using the OJT or "three-step" method.

Triple Net Lease —A lease providing that the tenant pay for all maintenance expenses, plus utilities, taxes, and insurance. This form of lease is particularly attractive to investors because of the limited exposure to liability. Investors will usually form an LLC or a limited partnership to own property.

Variance —A process of comparing actual result against preset standards and taking corrective action where needed.

Vision —Defines what you as owner what to achieve, over the long term, with your organization. It is usually expressed as a series of goals.

Worker's Compensation Insurance —Insurance required by law that compensates employees when they are injured on the job. The employer pays for worker's compensation insurance. It is done through your insurance company and is calculated as a factor of payroll. Your experience rating increases with claims.

Bilbliography:

McKeever, Mike. *How to Write a Business Plan:* Berkeley: NOLO, 2004

Sachs, Randi Toler. *How to Become a Skillful Interviewer:* New York: American Management Association, 1994

Arthur, Diane. *The Employee Recruitment and Retention Handbook:* New York: American Management Association, 2001

Abrahams, Jeffrey. *The Mission Statement Book:* Berkeley: Ten Speed Press, 1999

Kawasaki, Guy. *The Art of The Start:* New York: Penguin, 2004

Rabianski, Joseph S., James R. DeLisle and Neil G. Garn. *Corporate Real Estate Site Selection: A Community-Specific Information Framework:* Journal of Real Estate Research; July-October 2001 Volume 22 Issue ½ , page 165

Lawrence, Elizabeth. *The Complete Restaurateur A Practical Guide to the Craft and Business of Restaurant Ownership.* Penguin, 2001

Cannon, Howard. *Starting a Restaurant, 2nd Edition.* Penguin, 2005

Appendices

Mission Statements

Each word of your mission statement should create impact while utilizing as much economy with words as possible. Your mission statement should capture the essence of what "you" are and what your purpose is. Read the following for ideas:

Consider this early mission statement from **Nike:** "*Crush Reebok.*" And the more recent "*Just do it.*"

The following is a very powerful mission statement for **U.S. Special Operations Command** based at MacDill Air Force Base and composed of components from all four branches of American military each with special skills:" *To be the premier team of special warriors, thoroughly prepared, properly equipped, and highly motivated: at the right place, at the right time, facing the right adversary, leading the Global War on Terrorism, accomplishing the strategic objectives of the United States.*" Take a minute and pick that one apart. That is a beauty, a true work of art. That is a Statement of Mission.

Wal-Mart: "*To give ordinary folk the chance to buy the same thing as rich people.*"

Walt Disney: " *To make people happy.*"

Simple and to the point.

Coca Cola:

"*To refresh the world...in body, mind and spirit.*

"*To inspire moments of optimism...through our brands and our actions.*

"*To create value and make a difference...everywhere we engage.*"

I think that is a beautiful mission statement. It is lyrical and poetic.

NASA Mission Statement: *"To advance and communicate scientific knowledge and understanding of the Earth, the solar system, and the universe and use the environment of space for research. To explore, use, and enable the development of space for human enterprise. To research, develop, verify, and transfer advanced aeronautics, space, and related technologies."*

Levi Strauss & Co: *"People love our clothes and trust our company. We will market the most appealing and widely worn casual clothing in the world. We will clothe the world."*

Cooking With Gas, LLC: *"To be your Prophet for Profit."*

Each of these shows economy of words while conveying a world of information about that corporate entity. Make your mission statement pertinent. Beware that you don't sound glib or over promise. And as always, if we can be of assistance log on to www.cookingwithgas.net.

Records Retention Schedule:

	Retention Period
Corporate	
All Corporate records:	Permanently
Human Resources	
Applications (non-hires)	1 Year
Employee personal records: in house forms, performance appraisals, disciplinary actions, transfer, termination.	6 Years from date of termination
I-9 form	3 years from date of hire or 1 year after termination; whichever is longer.
Insurance policies (expired)	3 Years
Insurance Records: accident reports, claims etc.	Permanently
Garnishments	7 Years
Grievances Records	5 Years
Payroll Records; 940's, 941's w-4's	7 Years
Time Cards	4 Years
Financial:	
Accounting: Audit reports, Cash books, chart of accounts, disbursement journals, depreciation schedules, financial statements, general ledgers, journals, trial balances.	Permanently
Bank: Deposit Slips	2 Years
Bank: Reconciliations	2 Years
Bank Statements:	3 Years
Canceled Checks (Regular):	7 Years
Canceled Checks (checks for important payments of any type including property, assets, taxes etc. canceled check should be filed as attachment with related documents.):	Permanently
Expense Reports:	7Years
Invoices (vendor)	7 Years
Inventories	7 Years
Sales Records:	7 Years
Tax Returns:	Permanently
Miscellaneous:	
Property Records: Bills of Sale, deeds, mortgages, depreciation reserves and schedules, Blueprints, plans, permits etc.	Permanently
Material Data Safety Sheet (MDSS)	Permanently
Bills of lading, remittance advice, receiving Sheet:	1 Year

State Filing Requirements and Fees

For-Profit business entities.

Endnotes

[1] Some of the material for this section taken from *Staffing the Contemporary Organization*, by Donald L. Caruth and Gail D. Handlogten

[2] *Managing Organizational Behavior*, Fifth Edition: Schermerhorn, Hunt and Osborn

[3] If you are a multiple store operator, you will have inner store transfers IST's in which case you would add or subtract those items here.

[4] To calculate cost of condiments, take the cost of a unit, say a gallon, and then divide it by the number of sub units. Let's use the mustard in the example above. 1 gallon = 128 ounces, so with ½ ounce portions, you will have 256 portions of mustard. If a gallon of mustard costs you $6, then the mustard for one burger costs you .0234 cents. The same logic applies to the other condiments such as lettuce; one head costs $1.50 and covers 40 burgers. Lettuce for one burger costs .0375 cents.

[5] You know that because you divided total payroll dollars for last week by the number of hour worked.

[6] Organizational culture is a system of shared values, beliefs, customs and behavioral patterns within an organization.

[7] The panic or duress code is simply two different digits at the end of the code, so the bad guy doesn't notice. The system disarms just like usual, but the alert is sent to the central station.